MILITARY DOGS OF WORLD WAR II

Dedication

I wish to dedicate this book to the following family members who served in the armed forces:

Sgt. Thomas C. Bulanda, USMC, Ret., Iraq

Sgt. Bruce Ross, Ranger, G2, Army, Viet Nam

William Supko, Army, Viet Nam era

Ken van Dalen, Army, Viet Nam era

William Vitez, U.S. Navy, post-Korea

Steve Vitez, U.S. Army, Korea

George Vitez, U.S. Army, WWII

Stanley Bulanda, MoMM2C, USCG, WWII

Frank Bulanda, U.S. Army, WWII

Henry van den Broek, U.S. Army, WWII

Herman Ross, U.S. Army, WWI

CASEMATE | ILLUSTRATED

MILITARY DOGS OF WORLD WAR II

SUSAN BULANDA

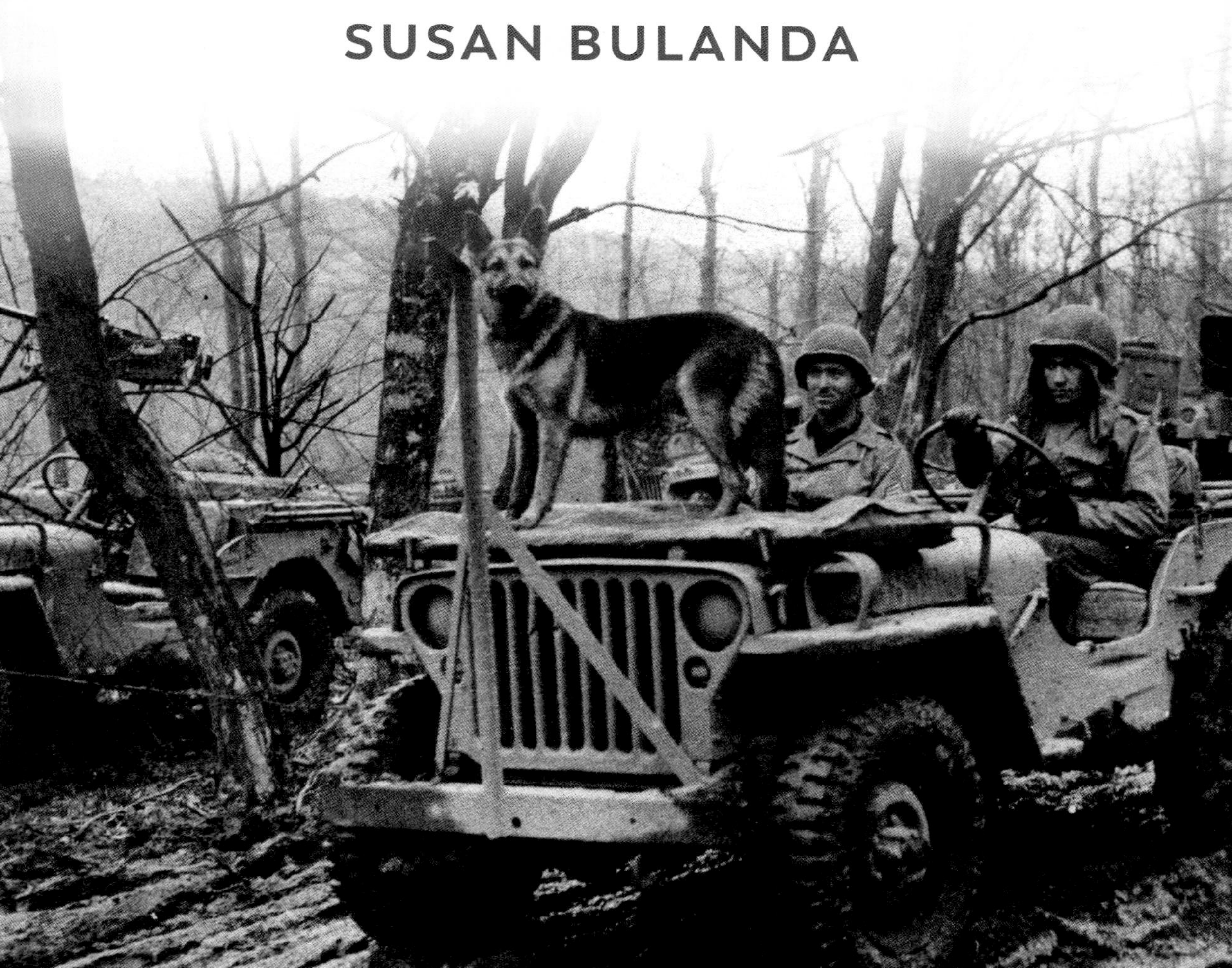

CASEMATE | ILLUSTRATED

CIS0035

Print Edition: ISBN 978-1-63624-325-2
Digital Edition: ISBN 978-1-63624-326-9

Design by Battlefield Design
Printed and bound in the Czech Republic by FINIDR s.r.o.

CASEMATE PUBLISHERS (US)
Telephone (610) 853-9131
Fax (610) 853-9146
Email: casemate@casematepublishers.com
www.casematepublishers.com

CASEMATE PUBLISHERS (UK)
Telephone (0)1226 734350
Email: casemate-uk@casematepublishers.co.uk
www.casematepublishers.co.uk

Title page image: This German Shepherd named Recall was captured from the Germans at St. Malo when he was only a few months old. He liked riding on the hood of the Jeep, Shevenhutte, Germany.

Contents page inset image: A Doberman stands guard while a soldier tries to sleep.

Contents page background image: Returning from a night patrol on Okinawa is Company G, 106th Regiment, 27th Division.

Acknowledgements: Few books are written in a void; therefore, I wish to acknowledge the help and support that I received from friends and family. First, my husband Larry who puts up with the hours that I spend on the computer. Next, I want to thank the members of the Black Diamond Writers Network, who always cheer me on, especially Steven Goodale of Gentle Slope Publishing, L.L.C. who reviewed my manuscript and suggested changes. No book can be a success without a great publisher and publishing team. Kudos to the Casemate Publishers team, especially Ruth Sheppard, Declan Ingram, Isobel Fulton, Daniel Yesilonis, Lizzy Hammond, Will Farnsworth, and Chris Cocks for making this book the winner that it is.

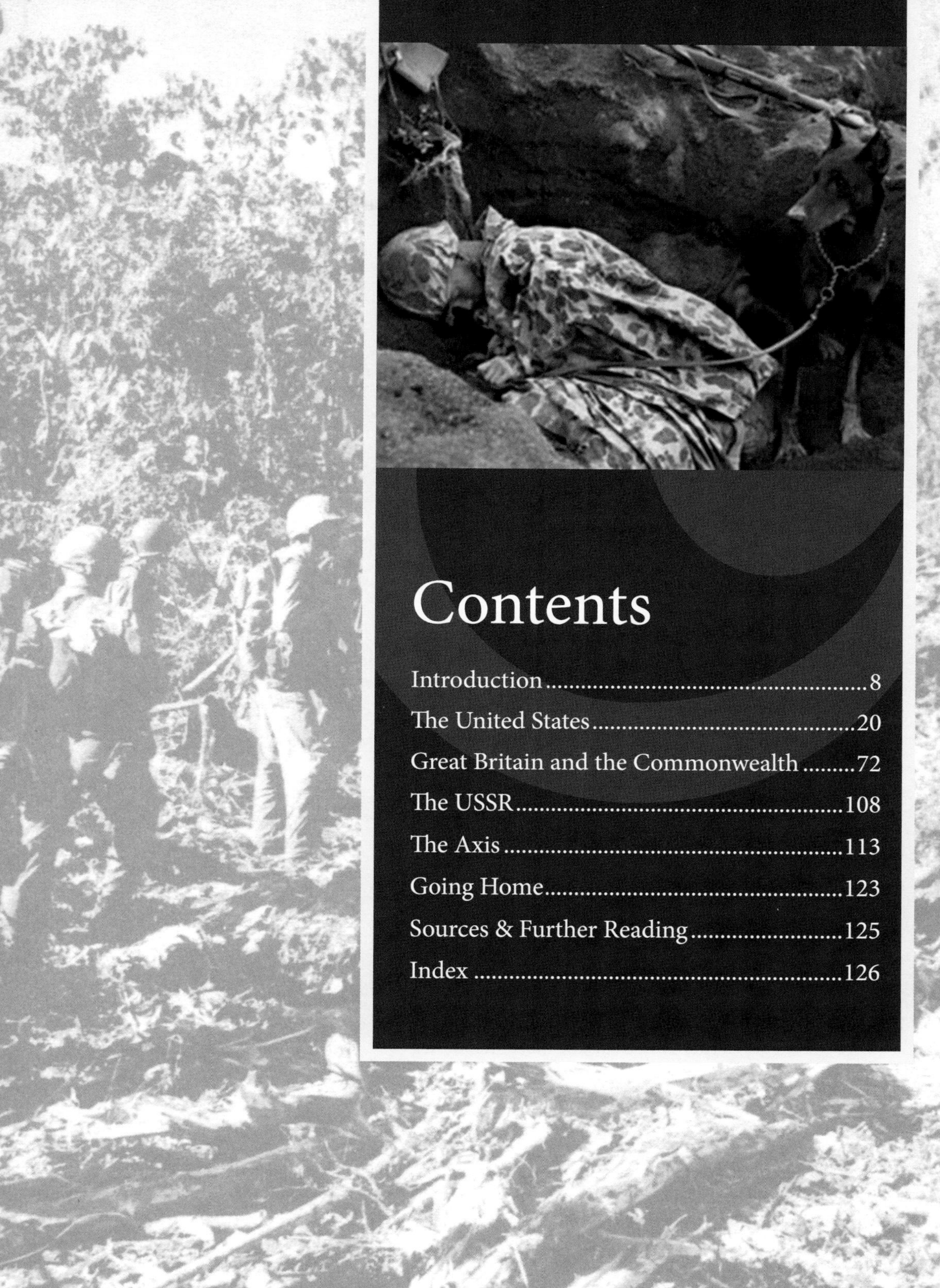

Contents

A French soldier bandages the paw of a Red Cross working dog in Flanders, Belgium, May 1917. (Photograph by Harriet Chalmers Adams, *National Geographic*)

Introduction

Animals have been a part of warfare for as long as there has been conflict, especially dogs, who have always been an important part of combat and have served in all wars since time immemorial. From ancient times, dogs were used in a wide variety of roles, many of which persist to this day, from actual fighting dogs used in combat to scouts, sentries, search and rescue dogs, messengers, trackers, and ambulance dogs.

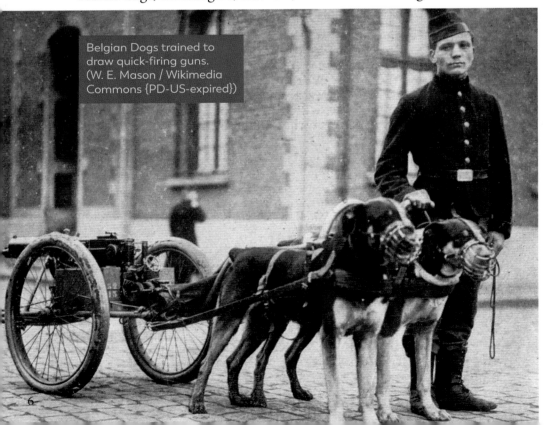

Belgian Dogs trained to draw quick-firing guns. (W. E. Mason / Wikimedia Commons {PD-US-expired})

The Greeks, Romans, Persians, Slavs, Sarmatians, and Britons all used dogs as a matter of course, mainly on sentry or patrol duty though there are accounts of dogs being taken into battle. There are records of dogs in warfare going back to the 7th century BC when Ephesian cavalry went into battle against the Magnesia, each accompanied by his war dog and a warrior bearing the spears. In an example of early psychological warfare, at the battle of Pelusium in 525 BC, Cambyses II had his troops array dogs, cats and other animals held sacred by his enemy, the Egyptians, in the front ranks in an effort to demoralize them and encourage them to cease throwing their javelins. In 480 BC, when Xerxes I, King of the Persians, invaded Greece, he took with him his vast packs of Indian hounds. In 120 BC, Roman consul Marcus Pomponius Matho used dogs from mainland Italy to hunt down Sardinian guerrillas hiding in caves during the invasion of the island. Attila the Hun is recorded using large war dogs in his campaigns of conquest. In the Middle Ages and beyond, Spanish conquistadors made extensive use of Mastiffs and other large breeds in the suppression of indigenous peoples. In the Far East, during the 15th century, Vietnamese Emperor Lê Lợi commissioned Nguyễn Xí to raise and train a pack of over 100 hounds. So impressed was the emperor that he promoted Nguyễn Xí to commander of a regiment of shock troops, accompanied by the phalanx of dogs.

During the Seven Years' War, Frederick the Great of Prussia made extensive use of dogs as messengers in the war with Russia. Napoleon used dogs in his campaigns, mainly in sentry roles. The first recorded use in the United States of dogs in a military role was in the Seminole Wars of 1816–58 in Florida. Dogs were used extensively by both sides in the Civil War as messengers, sentries, and for protection. General Ulysses S. Grant makes mention of the Union destroying Confederate and Southern bloodhounds because of their training in catching runaway slaves.

Sergeant of the Royal Engineers Signals Section putting a message into a cylinder attached to the collar of a messenger dog at Etaples, August 28, 1918. (Imperial War Museums, Q 9276)

German Red Cross dogs, 1914. (Bain News Service / Library of Congress CC0 1.0)

British messenger dogs with their handler, France, 1918. All three dogs would have been trained to carry messages between lines and command. Usually these dogs had been strays, so one particular breed of dog could not be preferred. Generally, however, traditional working breeds, such as Collies, Retrievers, or large Terriers, were chosen for messenger work. Messenger dogs were based in sectional kennels near the front lines. On average, each sectional kennel had 48 dogs and 16 handlers, a ratio that indicates how important the dogs' work was at the front. Before being shipped to France the dogs were trained at the War Dog Training School in Shoeburyness, England. (National Library of Scotland / Flickr CC0 1.0)

Into the more modern era, perhaps the "father" of the modern war dog was the German Jean Bungartz (1854–1934), a prolific and talented animal painter and author. In the 1880s he founded the *Hamburger Verein zur Förderung reiner Hunderassen*, the Hamburg Society of Pure-bred Dogs, before, in 1893, founding the *Deutschen Verein für Sanitätshunde,* the German Association of Red Cross Dogs, an organization that he led until 1909. At the time, France and Belgium were also developing their war dog programs. Belgium was using dogs in its military forces to tow heavy machine guns and light ordnance. Britain lagged behind and there was widespread resistance in the high command to implementing the use of dogs in warfare until around the turn of century, when Lieutenant-Colonel E. H. Richardson visited Germany to study under Bungartz. Richardson had witnessed the successful use of dogs in the British police force and felt there was a role for them in the military. He also visited France and Belgium to see first-hand their war dog programs. He returned to England and opened his kennels with his first dog, Sanita, which had been trained by Bungartz. On the outbreak of the Russo-Japanese War in 1904, Richardson supplied the Russians with two dogs trained in ambulance work; so successful did they prove that the British authorities finally sat up and took notice and Richardson established the UK War Dog program through World War I and even into World War II.

By the outbreak of World War I in 1914, all the belligerents were using military dogs in a variety of roles, from draft animals hauling machine guns and supply carts, to sentries and guard dogs, to messengers and couriers operating in the trenches—killing rats at the same time—under heavy fire. They were perhaps most valuable as mercy dogs in a paramedic role, locating wounded soldiers and working with search parties. These dogs are credited with saving countless lives. Many such dogs are now legendary, including the U.S. 102nd Infantry Regiment's Sergeant Stubby (1916–May 26, 1926), a highly decorated Pit Bull type who saw action in 17 major battles on the Western Front over a period of 18 months. On numerous occasions, he saved his unit from surprise mustard gas attacks as well as being a prolific mercy and ambulance dog.

A painting by Alexander Pope of a Red Cross dog carrying a soldier's helmet, August 1918. (https://redcrosschat.org)

Officers of German Flight Squadron 27, with their mascot, Bobby the French Bulldog, spring 1918. (DeGolyer Library, SMU Central University Libraries)

An ambulance dog at work on the Western Front, 1915. (W. E. Mason, *Dogs of all Nations*)

A casualty dog being trained how to jump over barbed wire.

The soldiers who worked with the war animals felt a special bond with them. This is true of soldiers, search-and-rescue personnel, and even the police of today. As a search-and-rescue dog trainer and handler, I have experienced the special bond that develops between a person and their working animal. People who use service animals also experience this deep, unwavering bond. This book is a glimpse of the many dogs that were used in World War II, as well as a brief history of some of the countries that used them. Some of the accounts of dogs in World War II are sadly cursory. This leaves us to wonder about the "rest of the story." However short the account is, it shows how much these animals meant to the men and women who worked with, owned, or knew them. With all that has been written about major conflicts, the fact that there are even brief accounts shows how much the animals meant to the writers.

It is important to note that the K9 war effort had a positive effect on the public. Prior to World War II, most dog owners did not formally train their dogs and did not belong to breed or obedience clubs. War dog training introduced the public to formal obedience

A casualty dog in training to find wounded soldiers and notify his handler.

A Marine "Devil Dog" being taught how to lead a patrol and detect the enemy. Note the dog is working on a harness.

A Marine dog practicing the high jump.

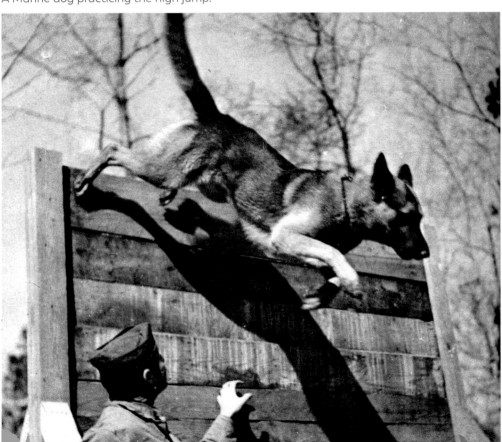

training: people were impressed with the performance of the dogs in the K9 Corps. Those who were fortunate enough to have their dogs returned to them were proud of the way the dogs now obeyed them. The dogs who made it through the Army's obedience program but did not make it through the advanced training were often returned to their owners, providing further examples of the benefits of obedience training. The training was a legacy that had a lasting effect on pet dogs in the years to come.

However, how dogs were treated and trained was based on the beliefs of trainers and scientists about the mind of the dog at the time. For the most part, dogs, and animals in general, were considered "dumb." Today we have ongoing research that illustrates the mental capabilities and *feelings* of dogs and other animals; this was not considered for the dog training programs of the two World Wars.

As late as the early 1970s, civilian dog training programs used the "jerk and hurt" method of training popularized by William Koehler. Some sporting dog trainers would pinch the ears and toes of dogs to make them do what was wanted. Reward was included, but in order to make a dog understand what was required, pain or discomfort was used to "teach" the dog what was expected. The general belief was that dogs only interacted with their environment through their instincts. Trainers took advantage of dogs' natural instinct to avoid pain by using choke chains, shock collars, and pinch collars, which are still used today.

A Marine dog being trained to attack the right arm to disarm the enemy. Note that the "victim" is wearing a full body padded suit.

However, not all trainers believed in harsh methods. Lieutenant-Colonel E. H. Richardson mentions in his books, more than once, that only kindness should be used to successfully train dogs.

Because the United States did not develop their war dog program, Dogs for Defense, until later in World War II, they needed to train dogs quickly so that they could field them as soon as possible. One of the key dog trainers was William Koehler, who used harsh methods to train dogs. For example, his method for training bomb- and mine-detecting dogs, which used traps to hurt the dogs if they got too close to the dummy bombs, was not as successful as the British method which used kindness instead of pain. Unfortunately, Koehler's methods were adopted after World War II for civilian and police dog training and continue to be used by some trainers to this day. However, more up-to-date dog trainers realized that dogs are much more intelligent than previously believed, that they have feelings, can do simple math problems, and solve other complex problems too. For a wonderful example of this, google "Chaser the Border Collie" and watch the video of him solving a difficult test.

As a result of the latest research, kinder and more successful dog training methods were developed in the 1990s and made popular by Karen Pryor, a Marine animal trainer who wrote the book, *Don't Shoot the Dog: The New Art of Teaching and Training.* As Pryor stated in one of her lectures, "You can't leash jerk a killer whale." Marine animals had to be trained using positive methods only. The result is the clicker training method used with dogs and other animals. Clicker training is a purely reward-based training method that I have personally and successfully used with dogs, cats, and birds.

Today, informed dog trainers and canine behavior consultants adhere to the LIMA training philosophy, which is the acronym for "Least Intrusive, Minimally Aversive." These professionals use the least intrusive, minimally aversive strategies in a set of humane and effective methods that are likely to be successful in training or implementing behavioral changes.

Many professional studies show that animals have a higher level of understanding, feelings, and intelligence than was understood previously. As we learn how to properly test animals, insects, and marine life, a new world is opened to us. Consider a discovery made by researchers at the University of California, San Diego, that honey bees have one of the most intricate forms of spatial referential communication outside of humans, and that it is a form of social learning. If bees have the awareness and intelligence to do this, imagine what dogs and other animals are capable of. Fortunately, we have come a long way since the War Dog program of World War II. It is exciting to think of the new discoveries about our beloved pets that we are yet to learn.

Wartime Roles

Ambulance Dogs

Ambulance dogs would search across a field or battleground looking for injured soldiers. If the soldier was capable, he would use the supplies in the pack on the dog's back. If he was mobile, the dog would lead the soldier to the field hospital. This was an important task because it would lessen the time it took for the soldier to get to where he could receive treatment. If the soldier was unconscious, the dog would take an item from the soldier, return to the medics, and then lead the medics to the wounded soldier. Dogs were also used by British firemen, civil defense personnel, police, and soldiers on the home front to locate people buried in bombed-out buildings.

Red Cross dogs also delivered carrier pigeons for communication.

Red Cross or casualty dogs were used to help wounded soldiers, either by providing first aid supplies in their packs, leading the wounded soldiers to medics, or leading medics to soldiers who were unconscious.

A communication dog ready to string wire. This dog is a third-generation from Rin Tin Tin, a famous dog trained by Corporal Lee Duncan, an aerial gunner in the U.S. Army Air Service. After the war, "Rinty" became an international star in silent films.

Communication Dogs

Communication or telephone dogs would travel with a reel of wire on their backs, or drag wire from a reel across the front lines or anywhere where communications were needed, as hard wired telephones were used by command posts to send secure messages to the field. As the command post and troops in the field moved, or if the wires were broken, they had to be reconnected. They also had a pack on their back with tools needed by the soldiers. This was especially important in mountainous or steep terrain, such as in Italy. Without these dogs, there may have been no reliable communications or no communication at all on some fronts. Dogs also carried crates of carrier pigeons to the front lines. While the use of pigeons in World War II was not as widespread as was the case in World War I, they were still used and, in some cases, were the most reliable means of communication available.

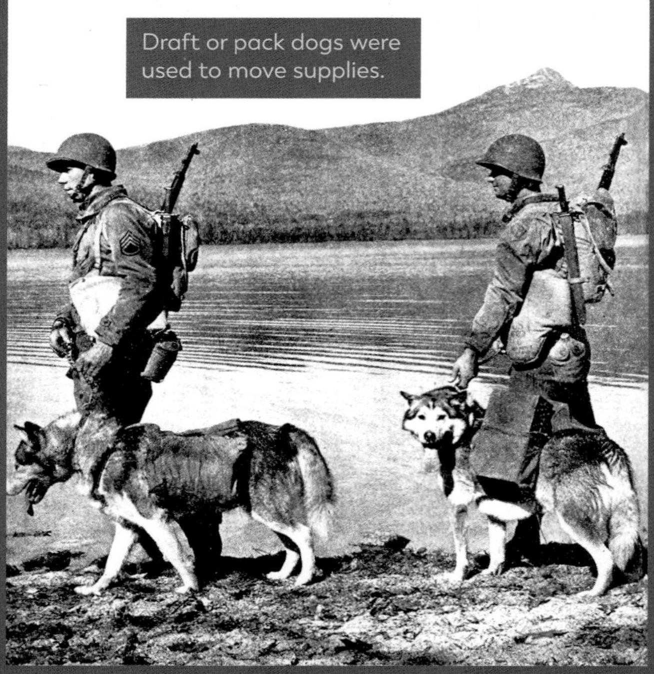

Draft or pack dogs were used to move supplies.

Draft/Sled Dogs

The use of draft dogs in World War II is one of the least celebrated jobs that was given to the dogs. Draft dogs would pull small supply carts—the German *Gebirgsjäger* or mountain troops used them to transport supplies. Elsewhere, large breeds such as Great Danes and Newfoundlands were used to carry supplies such as ammunition, pigeon coops, medical supplies, dry socks, food, water, telephones, and machine-gun parts.

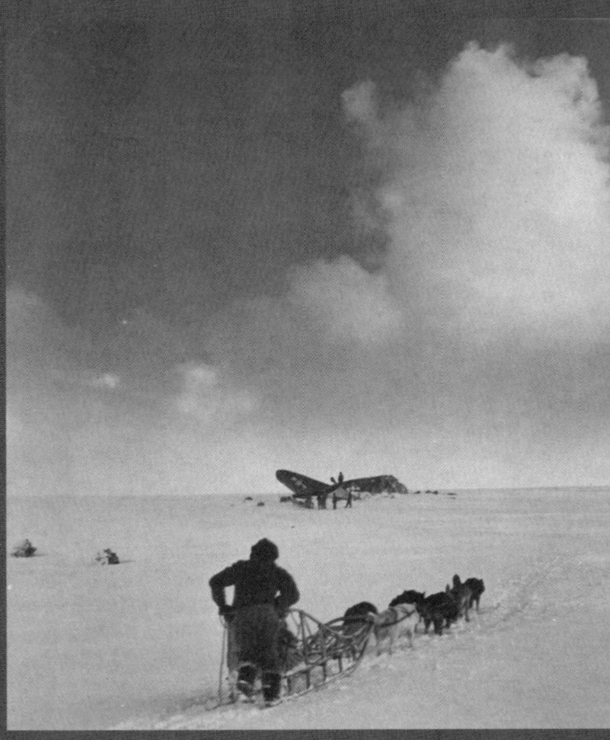

Alaskan Huskies pulling a sled towards a Douglas C-47 crash in Cathedral Valley, Alaska, c. 1945. (National Archives)

In both Canada and the U.S., dog sled teams were an essential part of finding and rescuing downed pilots, especially in the Arctic regions of Newfoundland, Greenland, Iceland, and Alaska which witnessed thousands of flights between the U.S., Great Britain, and the Soviet Union. These dogs would also carry supplies. Some draft dogs were also trained as paratrooper dogs. During the fighting in the Ardennes in the Battle of the Bulge, the rough terrain, deep snow, and thick forests made it very difficult, if not impossible, for medics to find and transport wounded soldiers. This was where the "paradogs" came into their own.

The survivors of the C-27 crash reach the bottom of the hill by dog sled. (National Archives)

Sentry Dogs

The Germans, British, and Americans all used sentry dogs on patrols. The dogs were taught to be silent and work about 30 to 40 yards in front of the soldiers. If the dog scented the enemy, they would point, or go back to the handler. These dogs are credited with saving many lives, and protecting command posts and important facilities. Often the enemy would try to infiltrate friendly lines or saboteurs would try to destroy depots, but they were compromised by the sentry dogs.

Most sentry dogs operated at night and were kept hidden during the day. They were used around strategic locations such as factories, bridges, beaches, and internment camps. The dogs would alert the handler to anyone in the area. In some cases, the dogs were turned loose to investigate and attack anyone they caught. These dogs were friendly, tail-wagging dogs by day, but when on duty they transformed into aggressive guard dogs.

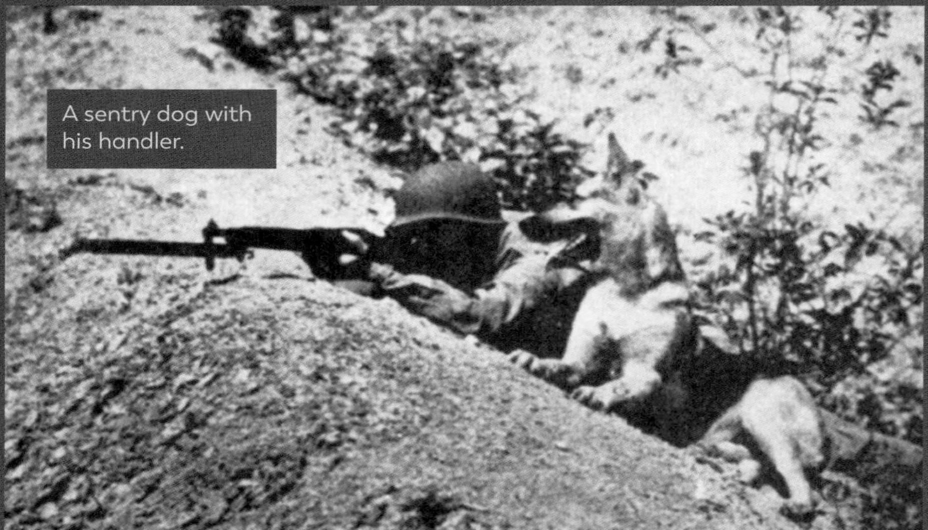

A sentry dog with his handler.

Mine-Detection Dogs

Because the new German plastic mines could not be detected by metal detectors, dogs were trained to find them. The dogs were taught to sit about 6 to 10 feet away from the mine. Unfortunately, dog trainers did not understand that a dog could detect the scent of the explosives, and instead taught them to look for disturbed soil. Since the weather would obliterate any disturbed soil, the success rate of the dogs was poor. Also, the dogs were distracted by battlefield debris and dead soldiers. It wasn't until after the war that dog trainers realized that dogs could detect the chemicals that made up the explosives.

Messenger Dogs

One of the most important jobs the dogs had during the war was as messengers. They carried metal cylinders with information, including maps, between front line units and headquarters. Again, these positions moved frequently so the dog had to remember where to go. American and British messenger dogs had two handlers per dog. One handler would stay at base while the other took the dog to its assigned area. When a message needed to be sent, the dog was told to report to his handler at base. The dogs were trained not to stop for anything along the way, to ignore other animals, people, and food. They were also taught not to be afraid of the sounds of battle, such as explosions and gunfire.

Messenger dog Prince returns with a message. Prince served with the 338th Infantry Regiment, 85th Division, and carried messages between the 2nd Battalion rear and the forward post.

The United States

At the start of World War II, Russia, Germany, Great Britain, and Japan had war dogs. The United States did not. The main reason for this was that the United States did not enter the war until Japan attacked Pearl Harbor. Even after the bombing, the American military did not feel that war dogs would be successful and refused to create a K9 unit.

Mrs Whitehouse Walker and Miss Blanche Saunders took it upon themselves to convince obedience clubs to train dogs for potential use in war. The following clubs contributed to this effort, focusing on training casualty, ambulance, and messenger dogs: the New England Dog Training Club under Bert D. Turnquist, the Long Island Dog Training Club under Mr and Mrs Harland Meistrell, and the Stockton English Springer Spaniel Training Club. Sentry dog training was sponsored by the Hartford Obedience Training Club. As the movement grew to provide the military with dogs, Dogs for Defense Inc. was created with the blessing of the American Kennel Club. Before dogs were used by the military, sentry dogs were employed by the Munitions Manufacturing Company in Poughkeepsie, NY.

Marines and Devil Dogs ready to head to the front lines at Guam.

K9 Corps Established

Finally, on March 13, 1942, the Army accepted the idea of using military dogs and commissioned 200 trained sentry dogs from Dogs for Defense. These dogs became the K9 Corps. For a dog to be accepted into the K9 Corps, he had to be between 1 and 5 years of age, stand more than 20 inches at the shoulder, weigh at least 50 pounds, be unafraid of repeated shooting and storms, be in good physical condition, and be aggressive, steady, and alert. Interestingly, field-trained hunting breeds did not work well as military dogs.

Dogs for Defense had some interesting and famous dogs donated to them. Troop K of the Hawthorne State Police Barracks in New York sent four of their famous Bloodhounds, which were expert man trackers: Danny Boy, Rusty, Tuffy, and Smarty. They were sent to Fort Robinson in Nebraska for their war dog training.

Famous actors and actresses sent their dogs, like Greer Garson's Poodle, Cliquot; Mary Pickford's German Shepherd, Silver; Bruce Cabot's Boxer, Frits; Rudy Vallee's Doberman Pinscher, King; and Ezio Pinza's, of opera fame, two Dalmatians, Boris and Figaro. One of the most famous dogs sent to Dogs for Defense decided to go AWOL. Duke, a Collie, who was the grandson of Albert Payson Terhune's Lochinvar Luck, was being processed at a garage in New York City when he broke free and ran off into Central Park. Two taxis filled with soldiers, the city police, and members of Dogs for Defense conducted the search for Duke. He was found 21 blocks from the garage and returned.

Preparing to head into the jungle at Luzon, Philippines.

A soldier and his dog find shelter on the beach at Leyte Island, Philippines.

At first, only purebred dogs were allowed in the program. However, due to the high demand, crossbreeds were permitted if their ancestry could be positively determined. Initially, more than 30 breeds were accepted by the K9 Corps. But as the Army trained these dogs, the breeds were narrowed down to German Shepherds, Belgian Sheepdogs, Doberman Pinschers, and short-coated Farm Collies (Border Collie types). Other acceptable breeds and mixes of these breeds included Bouviers des Flandres, Boxers, Briards, Alaskan Malamutes, Bull Mastiffs, Chesapeake Bay Retrievers, Curly Coated Retrievers, Dalmatians, Eskimos, Flat-Coated Retrievers, German Shorthaired Pointers, Giant Schnauzers, Irish Water Spaniels, Labrador Retrievers, Norwegian Elkhounds, Rottweilers, Siberian Huskies,

On patrol heading toward Balete Pass on Luzon.

Standard Poodles, Wirehaired Pointing Griffons, and Giant Schnauzers. The Army rejected giant breeds such as the Great Dane, along with some hunting breeds. Alaskan Malamutes and other Huskies were used as sled dogs.

The list of acceptable breeds shrank because it became apparent through training that some breeds did not work out, or were too rare to supply the Army in significant numbers. Finally, Dogs for Defense started their own breeding program but could not produce dogs fast enough. A call went out to the general public for dogs for the war effort, and many were donated. Donated dogs were examined and tested to see if they were suitable for military work. If the dog was rejected, he was sent back to his owner. All accepted dogs were sent to a training camp. If there was a small group of dogs, they were shipped by themselves. If there were ten or more dogs, they were accompanied by a military guard. Once they reached the training camp, they were examined again and given all necessary shots before being quarantined for two weeks. This was necessary because at that time not all dog owners vaccinated their dogs. After the two-week quarantine, the dogs were photographed and tattooed for identification. Each dog now had a complete set of records. Once that was accomplished, a certificate signed by the Quartermaster General was sent to the dog's owner.

Unlike the Marines and the Coast Guard, the Army was more open to using any breed of dog, believing that the breed did not matter as much as the dog itself. After the start of the K9 Corps, the Army asked Dogs for Defense to supply them with small breeds for detecting mines. These dogs included Cocker Spaniels, Fox Hounds, Basset Hounds, English Springer Spaniels, Otter Hounds, and Schipperkes. After a dog's training was completed and he had passed, the dog and his handler could be assigned to active duty anywhere in the world, and his life as a soldier began.

A new recruit being examined to see if he is suitable for service.

Walking the gangplank at Los Angeles, heading for the Pacific.

There were five dog training camps in the U.S.: the San Carlos War Dog Reception and Training Center in San Mateo California; the Fort Robinson Quartermaster Depot in Nebraska; the Front Royal Quartermaster Depot in Virginia; the Cat Island War Dog Reception Center in Gulfport, Mississippi; and Camp Rimini in Helena, Montana. Some training camps specialized in certain types of training. Cat Island Center focused on special detail work, such as training casualty dogs, and was used to train dogs for duty in the tropical South Pacific. It is important to note that loyal Japanese Americans helped to train these dogs by wearing captured Japanese uniforms, jumping out at the dogs while shooting guns with blanks, brandishing knives, or simply hiding for the dogs to find them.

Camp Rimini specialized in training sled and pack dogs due to the colder climate in Montana. Hawaii had its own dog recruitment and training center. This was due to the logistics of shipping dogs from Hawaii to other training centers.

Typical shipping crate for a military dog.

According to Blanche Saunders in *The Story of Dog Obedience*, the concept of obedience trials was adopted from the Associated Sheep, Police, and Army Dog Society of England. It was not until 1933 that the first "test," as it was called, took place. The second event was held in 1934. The test exercises included heeling on-leash and off-leash, sitting for two minutes, lying down for five minutes with the owner out of sight, a drop on recall, coming to sit in front of the handler, retrieving a dumbbell and then retrieving a lighter dumbbell over a jump. In 1936, the American Kennel Club (AKC) approved obedience as a sport. Until that time there was only one level of competition, but with AKC approval, the obedience competition was broken down into the three classes that we have today, Novice, Open, and Utility. It would appear that the military based their dog training programs on the AKC obedience programs, with modifications adapted for combat. However, obedience training for dogs to be used in war and police work was established prior to World War I. As mentioned, by 1884, the Germans had a military/war dog program, as did Lieutenant-Colonel Richardson in Britain prior to 1914. It is reasonable to assume that the U.S. knew about the successes and failures of these programs.

Military dog training was based on the master–dog relationship. Many of the K9 handlers were men who had experience with dogs, often as trainers or handlers. Training for the K9 handlers started with grooming, feeding, kenneling, disease prevention, and first aid. Next came the basic training as outlined in the military manual *TM 10-396 War Dogs*, July 1943. The training equipment was composed of: a 6-foot leather leash; a 25-foot lead; a chain choke collar; a leather kennel collar which was worn when not training; a chainette, also known as a throwing chain, which was used to correct a dog at a distance from the handler; a 3½-foot-high x 4-foot-wide hurdle; a muzzle; a gasmask; and a waterproof coat.

Dog training center.

Training for sentry dogs lasted eight weeks. All other specialized training took 13 weeks. Handlers were instructed to give commands firmly, and to always use the same command, to keep at it until the dog obeyed, and never let a dog ignore a command. They were also trained not to lose their temper or "get sore." The philosophy was that if your dog bit you it was your fault. Handlers only punished a dog if he did something wrong, and they were never allowed to hit the dog. Dogs were rewarded if they obeyed correctly by being given a pat on the head, being played with, or allowed do something they liked.

Basic obedience training started with the dogs on leashes and forming a line with the handlers. The dog was taught to stay on the handler's left side in a heel position so that the right hand was free to hold a weapon. Each dog/handler team was spaced six feet apart. The dogs were trained for about two hours twice a day.

The training starts with exercises that the dog already knows. After walking around a square several times, the dog is told to sit. The handler holds the leash in his right hand and will ease the dog into the correct sitting position with his left hand. The dog's shoulders are even with the handler's knee.

Once the dog knows the sit command he is taught to down on command. This is done by pulling down on the leash to show the dog to go down. The dog is expected to down on command from any position. Once the dog is in a down position and will hold it, he is told to go back to a sit position. When the dog has mastered the down command, he is taught to drop quickly into a down with the command cover, which involves both dog and soldier dropping to the ground to avoid attack. The handler and dog both drop quickly into the down position.

Stay is taught next. The dog is expected to hold the stay position until the handler returns and gives him a different command. The dog will either sit-stay or down-stay. At this point the dogs are walked around the square practicing the heel exercise.

The next exercise that the dogs are taught is to stay tied up quietly. The handler ties the dog to a post and walks a short distance away from but within sight of the dog. If the dog stays quiet for a minute the handler returns and rewards the dog. The length of time and distance that the dog is required to stay quietly tied up is gradually increased until the handler is out of sight of the dog.

Once the dog is solid with the stay exercise, he is taught to come on command. The dog is put in a down-stay and the handler backs away to the end of the leash. After waiting for a few seconds, the handler calls the dog's name and then immediately gives the command come. If necessary, the handler will gently tug on the leash to encourage the dog to come. When the dog arrives in the front of the handler the dog is told to sit. Once the dog sits, he is told to heel and guided into the heel position.

Crawl is the next exercise. The dog is expected to crawl alongside his handler or crawl toward his handler depending on the situation. The handler gives the dog the down command and then lies down next to the dog. Once they are in position the handler starts to crawl forward, encouraging the dog to crawl as well. Once the dog understands the command, the handler tells the dog to crawl from a distance.

The up/jump command is used to teach the dog to jump over an object. The dog is trained on a leash and taught to jump ahead of the handler. Once he clears the hurdle, the

A silent scout dog in training.

Coast Guard dog Brass practicing high jumps.

dog will return to the handler into a heel position. All types of hurdles are used, including walls that the dogs must scale.

Once the dog is proficient in all the exercises, the handler works the dog off-leash. As the dog improves, the distance between the dog and handler is increased so that the dog will respond to commands at a distance.

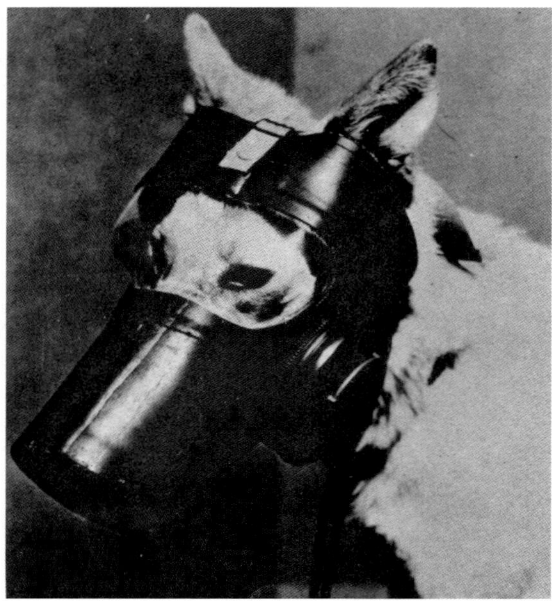

Additionally, the dogs are taught to be comfortable wearing muzzles and gasmasks. They are gradually introduced to these pieces of equipment until they are familiar with them. Because many dogs are unused to traveling in vehicles, they are also gradually introduced to different types of vehicles. The dog is required to ride quietly without becoming car sick.

As part of the advanced training, dogs are exposed to small-caliber gunfire from a distance. They are also exposed to the sound of explosions. Gradually, the volume of gunfire and explosions is increased so that the dog does not panic in battle situations.

The U.S. Army Chemical Warfare Service designed this gasmask for dogs.

97–98 QUARTERMASTER CORPS

CHAPTER 3

BASIC TRAINING

SECTION I

PRINCIPLES OF DOG TRAINING

97. General.—There are no tricks or mysteries to dog training. It is a relatively simple process if based on—

a. A practical knowledge of how a dog's mind works.

b. Constant repetition of training exercises.

c. Suitable recognition of a dog's progress.

d. Patience.

98. Basic principles.—The effectiveness of a dog training program depends on the regard shown for certain basic principles.

a. The trainer must establish himself as the master of the dog or dogs assigned to him. He pets, praises, feeds, and handles only the dog or dogs assigned to him; he does not permit any individual other than himself to make friends with the dog or dogs assigned to him.

56

A list of exercises as outlined in *TM 10-396 War Dogs.*

Sit on-leash. The dog is taught to sit when the soldier stops and the dog is in the heel position.

This dog is practicing how to heel on-leash with his shoulders almost even with the handler's knee.

Drop on command. After the dog is taught to down, he is taught to drop on command with a hand signal.

The dog is taught to stay both on- and off-leash using a hand signal.

The crawl exercise. The dog is to crawl either beside the handler or on command by himself.

The training manual set out in detail what was required of the handlers who would be training dogs:

QUALIFICATIONS OF TRAINING PERSONNEL

Essential traits. – Successful care and training of dogs depends to a great extent on personal characteristics of the trainers. Experience has shown that the following traits are essential:

a. Friendly attitude toward dogs. – Any individual selected for the training of dogs should be sympathetic and friendly toward dogs. This is a primary requisite.

b. Intelligence. – It has been demonstrated that individuals with less than average intelligence cannot be taught to care for and train dogs successfully.

c. Patience and Perseverance. – The trainer cannot force desired behavior upon dogs nor can he expect dogs to learn as readily as human beings. He must therefore be patient, and he must persevere until each exercise is brought to a successful conclusion.

d. Mental and physical coordination. – A good trainer must be able to convey his wishes to the dog by body movement and gestures as well as by voice. This requires a definite amount of mental and physical coordination.

e. Physical endurance. – Not only must the trainer be able to show good coordination, he must also be able to maintain his efforts as long as necessary. The trainer must "outlast" his dog during each training period.

f. Resourcefulness. – Although training procedure has been carefully set forth in this manual, it is inevitable that situations will arise calling for action not covered by rules.

g. Dependability. – The welfare of the dog is entirely in the hands of the trainer or master. Dogs cannot tell how they are being treated nor can they make reports. Their physical well-being depends, furthermore, on the willingness of the trainer or master to do such manual labor as is necessary for kennel management, feeding, and dog cleanliness. Failure in these responsibilities means failure of the training program.

Excerpt from the training manual explaining some training philosophies.

Group exercises. As part of basic obedience training, the dogs and handlers are to walk in a line around a square area.

Down on command at a distance off-leash. The dogs are taught to drop down on command, eventually following the down command at a distance.

Teaching the dog to jump on command. The up or jump lessons start with a lower obstacle. The dog is taught to jump over an obstacle in front of the handler instead of alongside.

Advanced jump or scaling an obstacle. The dogs are taught to up or jump over obstacles. In this photo the dogs are practicing off-leash jumping/scaling.

A military patrolman checking essential rolling stock that transported supplies.

Draft/sled dogs were used in many cases where vehicles were virtually useless. To solve this problem, Colonel Norman Vaughan flew 200 sled dogs and their mushers from their Arctic command posts to parachute into the needed areas. The Army dismissed the idea initially, but when Lieutenant-General George S. Patton approved it, the plan was initiated. Search-and-rescue stations were part of the Air Transport Command of the United States Army Air Forces, and established units of Malamutes, Huskies, Eskimo and mixed-breed Huskies in Greenland, Canada, Presque Isle, Maine, and Alaska. The North Atlantic Wing had over 300 sled and pack dogs under its command.

If a plane went down in an area where another plane could not land, the rescue crews would fly a dog team to the closest accessible location to the downed plane. The mushers would then dog sled to the downed plane. Eventually, the military would parachute a dog team to the location of the downed plane. An example of a daring rescue by a sled dog team was when an RAF Ferry Command crew had to land their bomber on thin ice in Greenland. The team of Huskies and Eskimos were flown as close as they could get to the bomber and were able to save the men and important equipment just before the plane sank into the icy water.

It is sad to say that the method of training mine-detection dogs by the United States was based on cruelty. It involved making the dogs associate fear and pain with mines. The man responsible for this method was William "Bill" Koehler. The method involved placing six steel game traps around the mine. The handler would work toward the mine and let the dog's foot or feet step into a trap, so that the dog associated pain with the mine. To ensure that this method worked, the traps were left on the dog's foot for eight to 10 seconds. If this did not work, the dog was allowed to step on electrified wire buried in the ground next to the mine. When the U.S. sent their mine dogs overseas, they were successful only 30 percent of the time. This was due in part to the dogs associating turned earth with electric shocks.

In England, Richardson stated emphatically that you could not use harsh methods to successfully train dogs to perform the complex tasks that they needed to do. While they did not use clicker training per se, they did use a form of positive training. The fact that Richardson said not to use harsh methods implies that harsh methods did exist and that some people used them. Because of Richardson's influence on training methods for dogs, the British had a 51 percent success rate with their mine-detection dogs compared to the Americans' 30 percent because they were rewarded with meat instead of being punished. The British mine dogs, trained by the Royal Engineers, were the first to be used to detect non-metallic landmines. It is a credit to the war dogs that they were able to work successfully on their own and were able to adapt to the changing circumstances as needed.

Sled dogs on the Western Front that were part of the Arctic Search and Rescue Unit, North Atlantic Wing. Note the airplane in the upper left. The dogs were flown in to transport wounded soldiers. Typically, the dogs were flown from Iceland in C-47s. Most of the dogs appear to be Siberian Huskies.

Chips

One of the more famous dogs in World War II was Chips, who was the most decorated dog in the war. Chips was a mixture of German Shepherd–Collie–Siberian Husky, donated by his owner, Edward J. Wren. According to Clayton G. Going, "Chips joined the K9 Corps because he bit a garbage man! And within a year this German Shepherd saw action in North Africa and Sicily, met President Franklin D. Roosevelt and Prime Minister Winston Churchill, was recommended for the Distinguished Service Cross, won the Silver Star, and bit General Dwight D. Eisenhower."

His first assignment was a very important one, guarding the Anfa Hotel in Casablanca where Roosevelt and Churchill were having a conference. Chips was handled by Private John P. Rowell of the 30th Infantry Brigade, 3rd Infantry Division, as part of the Western Task Force under Major-General George S. Patton, Jr. Chips and Rowell served in North Africa, Sicily, Italy, France, and Germany.

Chips and two other dogs, Watch and Mena, were the first American war dogs to land on D-Day at Fedala, 12 miles from Casablanca, as part of the U.S. Army's Center Attack Group, Operation *Torch*, in November 1942. Chips amazed the troops who served with him with his intelligence and bravery. For example, while he and his handler were pinned down on a beach in Sicily, Chips left his handler, jumped into the machine-gun pillbox and attacked the machine-gunners, forcing the four Germans inside to surrender. Chips only suffered

Chips meets General Eisenhower.

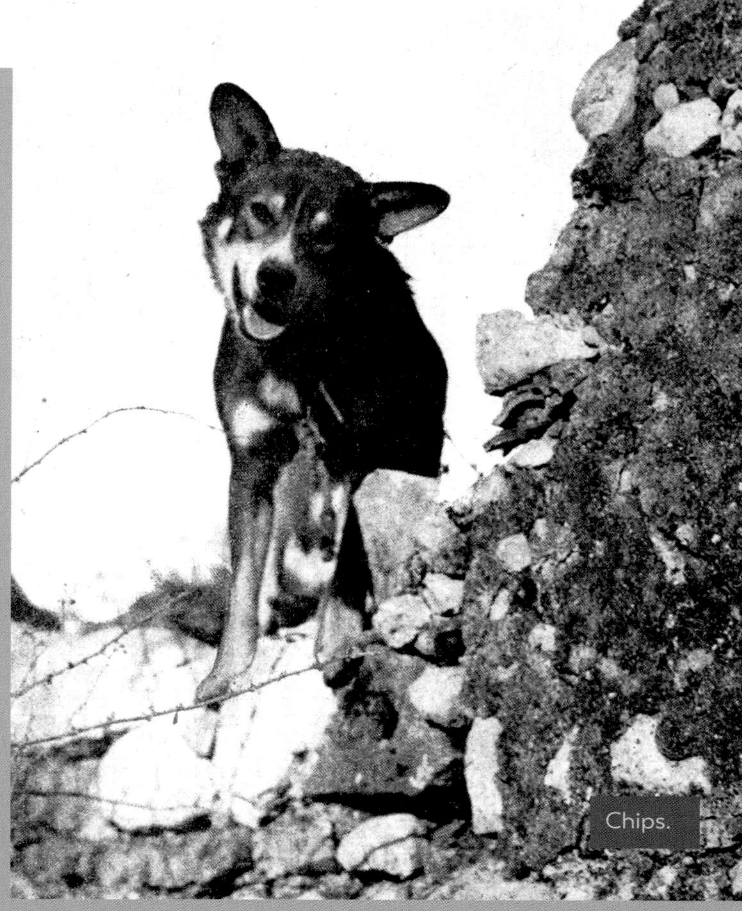
Chips.

minor injuries. Later the same day, he helped capture ten Italian soldiers. Chips was awarded the Purple Heart because a machine-gun bullet had grazed his scalp and he had powder burns on his fur.

When Rowell became sick, Chips was assigned to Sergeant William Haulk. They continued to serve together until December 1943. In a letter to Chips's owner, Haulk wrote, "Chips has been with us through all our combat in Italy. In the last few weeks, however, Chips has grown kind of nervous of shellfire, so we have had him transferred to our division headquarters where he is doing guard duty for our commanding general. Although we miss him very much in the company, we know he deserves the break. We hope to get him back after the war is over and keep him until he is returned to you." Another soldier, Private Charles R. Zimmerman, who served with Chips in Africa, Sicily, and Italy, also wrote to Chips's owners, "He still likes to run after bicycles and does not like a man or woman that he does not know. He did not like the French or Arabs at all. Your Chips is a dog to be proud of and every member of the battalion that he is in sure is proud of him. I am glad that we have Chips and dogs like him on our side instead of the enemy's."

Even though the dogs were trained to work under shellfire and gunfire, they too had encounters that caused them to suffer what was referred to at that time as "shell shock" and today as Post-Traumatic Stress Disorder, or PTSD.

Marine Devil Dogs

The Marine Corps preferred Doberman Pinschers, which became the official breed for the Corps. As soon as the call went out, the Doberman Pinscher Club started a nationwide recruiting program headed by Richard C. Webster of Baltimore, Maryland.

Group training exercise.

The dogs earned the name "Devil Dogs" after the nickname that the Germans gave the U.S. Marines during World War I. Even though the Marines preferred Doberman Pinschers over other breeds, they also used German Shepherds.

The Marines learned at Bougainville that their dogs needed to have a stable temperament. They preferred dogs that were 25 inches at the shoulder and about 60 pounds in weight. This size was ideal for the type of work that they had to do. Keep in mind that if a dog was wounded, the soldier would have to carry the dog back to base. The military likes regulations and aims to keep things standardized. Even the Marines had to be a certain height and weight as well as being healthy. The Marines also discovered that bitches were not as desirable since they often did not have the temperament to withstand the noise and confusion of explosions and gunfire.

The success of the Devil Dog program can be attributed to a schoolteacher named Clyde A. Henderson, who taught chemistry at the James Ford Rhodes High School in

Unloading a Devil Dog from the ship, Marshall Islands.

Unloading a Marine Devil Dog off the coast of Guam from a landing craft to an Alligator.

Cleveland, Ohio. Henderson was also an amateur dog trainer and a judge at obedience trials, as well as chairman of the training committee for the Doberman Pinscher Club of America, president of the Doberman Pinscher Club of Greater Cleveland, and a member of the board for the Western Reserve Kennel Club. Because of his success in the organization and recruitment of dogs for the Marine War Dog program, he was offered a first lieutenant's command to join the Marines and run their dog training program. Needless to say, he accepted.

A Marine dog earned ranks according to his length of service:

Three months of service = Private First Class

One year = Corporal

Two Years = Sergeant

Three Years = Platoon Sergeant

Four Years = Gunner Sergeant

Five Years = Master Gunner Sergeant

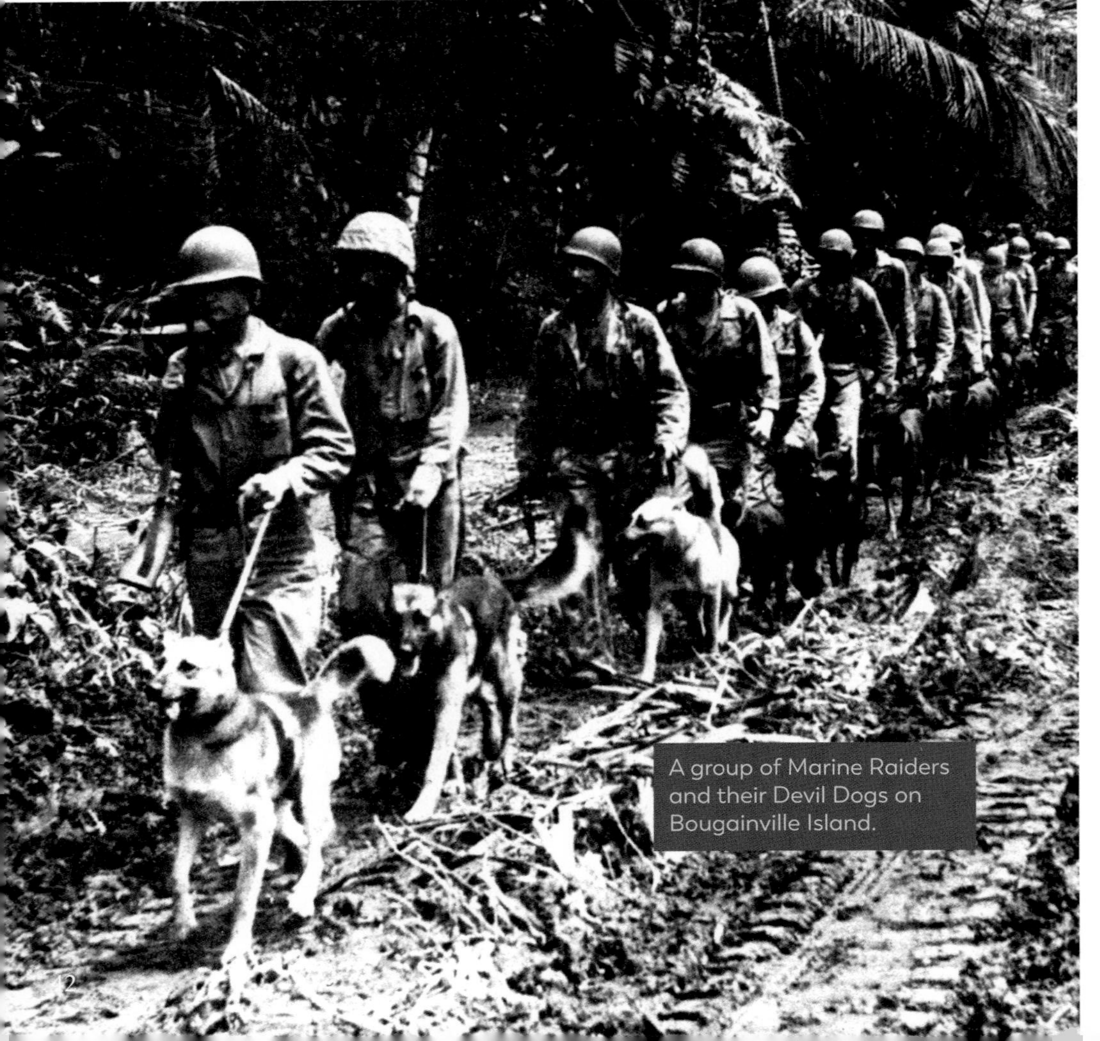

A group of Marine Raiders and their Devil Dogs on Bougainville Island.

An American patrol in the jungle of New Britain, New Guinea.

Marine Devil Dogs were taught two jobs, scout and messenger work. The scout dogs worked ahead of the patrols or larger units. When the dog found the enemy, the handler told the dog to "down" while the soldiers in the unit fanned out to look for the enemy. The dog and handler then retreated to the safest area possible.

Messenger dogs not only carried messages, but ammunition and medical supplies to the front lines and maps to the rear command posts. They were noted for being very fast and had been clocked doing a mile in four minutes. Keep in mind that this was not done on a smooth paved road or path, but in the terrain and vegetation of the jungle.

The Devil Dogs would attack if necessary and were trained to go for the arm holding a weapon. They were taught to release on command as well. They were never taught to kill a man. The dogs were also taught to crawl with their handler. They were taught to never bark, since it would give away the soldier's position, and never to show gun shyness.

Bougainville is a large island part of Papua New Guinea. It is rainforest with mostly inactive volcanos. Earthquakes are frequent but typically do not cause damage. There is a wide variety of tropical birds and bats. It rains almost every day and because of the heat and moisture, it is very humid. The lush vegetation made movement difficult. The Marine Dog Platoon first made history in Bougainville, saving many lives while securing the beachhead.

Note the Devil Dog straining on the leash, indicating that he has found a hidden Japanese soldier on the coast of New Guinea.

Marine reinforcements on Peleliu Island. Note the Marine and his Devil Dog on the right. Patrols that had a dog in the lead rarely lost a man.

Before the Marines and dogs landed towards the end of 1943, the Japanese positions were bombarded by ships offshore. After that, American planes flew over the island dropping bombs and strafing Japanese positions. At the same time, smoke was pouring forth from an active volcano. However, the Japanese were still dug in and as the Higgins boats with the Marines and dogs sped to shore, the Japanese began launching mortar shells at the boats. It is impossible to imagine what the dogs might have felt. It was rough for the soldiers, but the noise had to be deafening to the dogs' sensitive ears. The smell of cordite and explosives would also have been unpleasant and the shockwaves from the enemy mortars and the American shells overhead must have been very disturbing. Yet the dogs did not flinch, even as enemy machine-gun bullets pinged against the sides of the boats.

On patrol, the dogs alerted the Marines to ambushes and snipers. The success of the dogs was demonstrated by the fact that if a patrol was led by a dog, the patrol rarely suffered casualties, and the Japanese were not able to infiltrate Marine positions that had guard dogs.

The Dogs of Bougainville

Bougainville in the Solomon Islands was heavily occupied by 65,000 Japanese troops. The Japanese needed Bougainville to protect Rabaul, the major Japanese garrison and naval base in Papua New Guinea. However, there were only a few Japanese troops occupying the western part of the island. The area around Cape Torokina in the west was therefore used by the Americans for their staging area. There was no airfield, but the Empress Augusta Bay provided a safe anchorage. The area was surrounded by thick jungle and mountain ranges, making an attack by the Japanese difficult. The Marines needed time to establish a strong perimeter around the area where they planned to build an airfield.

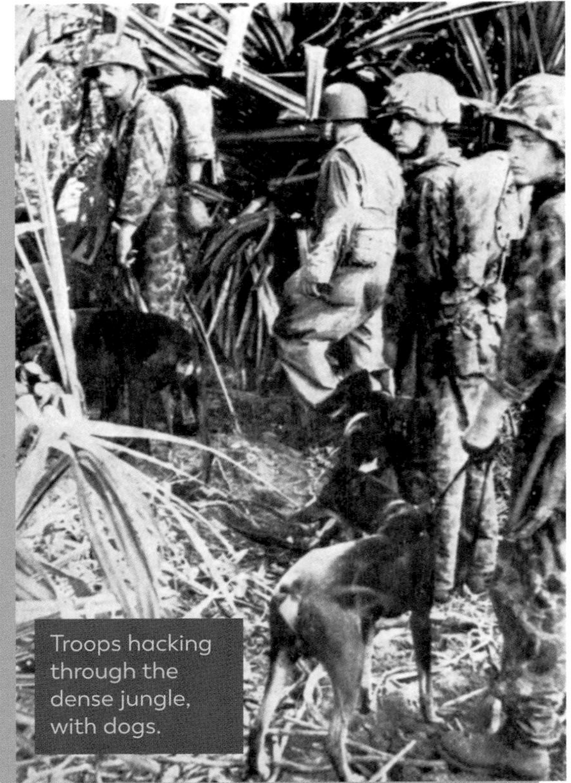

Troops hacking through the dense jungle, with dogs.

On Bougainville at Empress Augusta Bay, Marine Raiders pass a machine-gun nest, a place where machine-guns and soldiers were hidden, as they travel through the jungle.

The K9 company on Bougainville consisted of 52 men and 36 dogs. Noted for their outstanding service were four Doberman Pinschers, a Belgian Shepherd, and a German Shepherd, all donated to the Marines by their owners. The dogs had a variety of duties which included sending messages, laying wire for communications, detecting ambushes and snipers, and being alert to machine-gun nests and enemy patrols.

Rex

Rex was a Doberman Pinscher scout dog. It had been a dismal, hot, humid night. Rex was lying next to his handler who was trying to get some sleep when suddenly his body stiffened, and he gave a deep growl. Instantly, his handler awoke and alerted the rest of the Marines. The men fully trusted Rex and quietly prepared for the attack that they knew was coming. Through the jungle, the Japanese silently crept toward the Marines. Their shadows moved slowly, difficult to see through the humid air, but the Marines were ready; they were able to repel the Japanese successfully.

Otto

Otto, a Doberman Pinscher scout dog, was leading a reconnaissance patrol. Things had been going smoothly until Otto froze on the trail and pointed to a spot 100 yards away. Instantly, the Marines dove for cover and seconds later a Japanese machine gun opened fire. The Marines regrouped and were able to take out the machine-gun nest.

Andy

Doberman Pinscher Andy became famous for his part in the landing at Empress Augusta Bay. The invasion caught the Japanese by surprise and the Marines leading the operation determined that the Japanese would try to bring up reinforcements. Within two hours of the landing, the Marines had set up a roadblock on the Piva Trail to stop the Japanese from advancing. The trail was overgrown and thick with vegetation that provided cover for the enemy. The Marines had to hack their way through the trail. There had not been time to

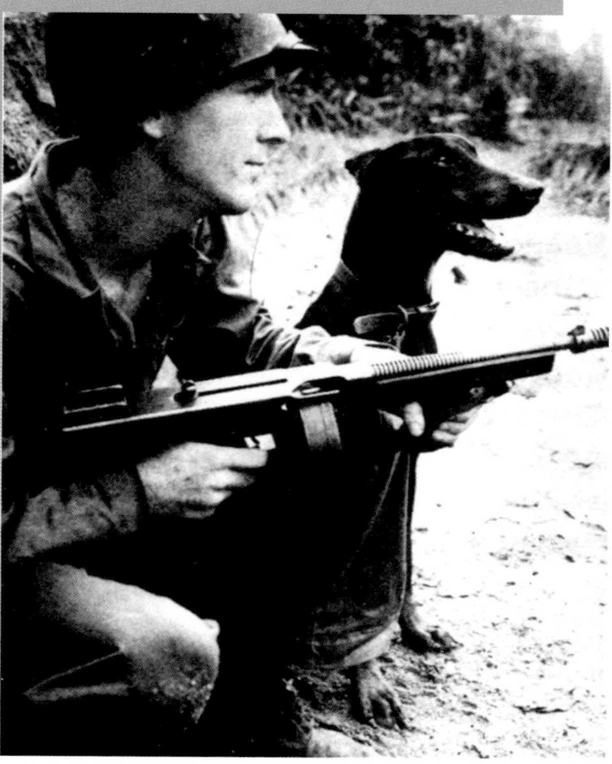

Andy the Doberman, part of the Empress Augusta Bay operation.

clear the area of any hidden Japanese. Andy and his two handlers, PFC Robert E. Lansley, who was known as a daredevil in his own right, and PFC Jack Mahoney, were assigned to lead the company. Snipers and ambushes were always a threat.

Andy was working off-leash about 25 yards in front of the 250 Marines. Normally, Andy would walk in a relaxed manner as a dog would on a stroll, but if he detected the enemy, he would stop, freeze, and the hair on his back would rise. Three times on that patrol Andy alerted and the Marines were able to take cover and identify the hidden Japanese. One of those times was a very close call for Andy's handlers. Andy froze, the men hit the ground, and machine-gun bullets whizzed just a few feet over their heads.

A few weeks later, after his initial patrol on the Piva Trail, Lansley got news of a patrol that had gone up the trail to establish an advanced position and was being held up by the Japanese. Without permission, Lansley, Mahoney, and Andy decided to go and help them. The danger was evident when on the way they came across a dead Marine who had been knifed. A few seconds after finding the dead Marine, Andy gave an alert, indicating enemy troops on both sides of the trail. Lansley told his partner to cover him while he crept forward to find the enemy. He opened fire with his Tommy gun to lure the Japanese into the open but discovered more than one machine-gun nest. A bitter firefight ensued but just then, four Marine light tanks moved up to assist the beleaguered Marines. The area was cleared but Lansley had been wounded in the chest by a hand grenade. Mahoney was evacuated to a field hospital, suffering wounds to his shoulder, back, and hand. Andy was unhurt.

Caesar

Caesar was a unique dog. He was owned by a family of five in the Bronx who lived on the fourth floor of an apartment building. If the mother needed something from the store, one of the boys would take Caesar with him, make the purchase, and then give the package to Caesar and tell him to "take it to mom." Caesar would carry the package back to their apartment, never stopping until he reached home. Caesar was donated to Dogs for Defense and sent to the Army training facility. Next, he went to Camp Lejeune to be trained as a Devil Dog messenger dog. He was assigned to the same company as Andy the Doberman Pinscher and served at Bougainville.

Caesar.

Caesar with his handler PFC Rufus Mayo on Bougainville Island.

A roadblock had been established by the Marines on the Piva Trail but the Japanese had cut the phone line that the Marines had stretched from the advanced position to headquarters. Caesar was now the only means of communication with headquarters. Caesar's two handlers were PFC John Kleeman and PFC Rufus Mayo. One night, Caesar and one of his handlers, PFC Rufus Mayo, were bedded down in a foxhole. Suddenly, Caesar woke Mayo just in time for him to hear the click of a hand grenade. Mayo was able to quickly grab the grenade and throw it in the direction it had come from. The next morning, they found eight dead Japanese soldiers. The Japanese liked to sneak up on the Marines at night. On another night, as Mayo and Caesar were asleep in a foxhole, a Japanese soldier tried to sneak up on them. Before Mayo was fully awake, Caesar heard the man coming and leaped out of the foxhole to attack him. Mayo called Caesar back but as he turned, the Japanese soldier shot the dog twice.

Caesar was able to make it back to the battalion command post where his wounds were treated. He was carried out of the jungle to the regimental headquarters on a stretcher. The Marines saluted him as he went by.

In training as an attack dog.

Rolo

Rolo, a Doberman Pinscher, was born on December 7, 1941, destined to become a Marine Devil Dog. His picture was hung in the Federal Museum of the United States Subtreasury Building, with a newspaper account of his service. It was on the steps of this building that Rolo was inducted into the military. Like Andy and Caesar, Rolo fought at Bougainville. Rolo's two Marine handlers were PFC Russell T. Friedrich and PFC James M. White.

The Army had assigned a patrol to work with the Marines at Bougainville and assigned Rolo to lead it along the Torokina River. When they were about 3,000 yards into the jungle, Rolo gave an unmistakable alert, pinpointing an enemy position about 75 yards ahead. However, the patrol leader did not believe Rolo's alert and ordered Friedrich and Rolo to continue the advance. But the soldiers in the patrol had heard the Japanese calling "Doggie, doggie" and started talking among themselves. Just after Friedrich had called Rolo back and sent him back to White to keep him out of danger, the bullets started flying. The Japanese were intent on killing Rolo and both handlers were caught in the crossfire. White was positioned in tall grass and Friedrich had taken cover eight feet away, behind a tree. As the bullets got closer to White and Rolo, White sent Rolo back to Friedrich for better cover. As Rolo crawled away and almost reached Friedrich, he was hit and killed instantly. Friedrich was also hit, while White took a bullet that went through his helmet and grazed his scalp. The attack was so intense that the patrol was forced to withdraw. When they regrouped and returned to the area, they found Rolo's body but not Friedrich's. They assumed he had been taken prisoner. Not believing Rolo's alert had cost the lives of Marines and a gallant dog.

Jack the Belgian Shepherd

Two Marine dogs with the same name were Jack, a Belgian Shepherd, and Jack, a Doberman Pinscher.

Jack, the Belgian Shepherd, was light brown with white patches. Ironically, he had been left at a shelter by his former owner who had joined the Army. Jack had originally been adopted by a loving family and was known for his exploits around town. His favorite was to steal an ice-cream cone right out of the hand of a child. Of course, his owner always made good, and the townsfolk loved Jack because he was always gentle.

Jack and his handlers, PFC Paul Joseph Castracane and PFC Gordon J. Wortman, were part of the Marine contingent that landed at Bougainville. It was only seven days into the invasion that Jack and Wortman were wounded. The team had been assigned to the roadblock on the Piva Trail and because the Japanese had cut the phone lines, all communications had to be via messenger dogs. The roadblock was under fierce Japanese attack and the Marines were taking casualties. Wortman had been shot in the leg and a machine-gun bullet had hit Jack in the back; although Jack cried with pain, he did not run but stayed

Sentry dog training.

with Wortman. Jack was the only dog the Marines had available to send a message for desperately needed help. Wortman and Jack were laying on the ground, under cover, when an officer crawled over to them and explained that Jack was their only hope. Wortman took the message and put it in the pouch under Jack's neck. With all the confidence in the world, he stroked Jack's head and whispered to him to report to Paul. Jack whimpered and slowly got up. Then, like a shot, he raced into the jungle as the Japanese tried their best to shoot him.

Jack made it back to the battalion command post and collapsed at his handler's feet, blood gushing from his wound. The Marines at the roadblock received the reinforcements they needed, and many lives were saved, including that of Wortman. Jack eventually made it back to the United States, where he was hailed as a war hero.

Jack the Doberman

Jack was assigned to PFC Carl L. Robertson and PFC Nick Barach, Jr., and was also a Devil Dog on Bougainville. On the eighth night that Jack had been on Bougainville, he kept alerting both his handlers. They did not hear or see anything and did not take Jack's alerts seriously. Jack kept pointing to a tree that was located near the command post. In the morning, Robertson pointed out the tree to another Marine, explaining that Jack kept indicating it. The Marine aimed his rifle at the tree, fired, and a Japanese sniper in full camouflage gear fell to the ground. It was obvious that the sniper had been waiting to shoot high-ranking officers in the command post. Jack's handlers never questioned his alerts again.

Liney

Liney, a Doberman assigned to PFC Robert S. Forsythe and Pvt. Reaymond E. Genay, was known for being a scrappy dog who would get into fights with other dogs and bite people. Liney and his handlers were assigned to Bougainville where the dog had quite a career.

On one patrol the Marines were investigating a report of enemy activity in dense jungle vegetation, with Liney leading the patrol. Suddenly, he gave a

Liney and PFC Robert S. Forsythe.

strong alert and the Marines dropped to the ground. They saw eight Japanese soldiers sitting in the open. They had stumbled on a Japanese stronghold and for three hours the battle raged. After the fight, they returned to base to regroup and then went deeper into the jungle with Liney in the lead again. The Marines found another Japanese stronghold, and because of Liney's alerts, were able to initiate a surprise attack. During that battle, Liney and his handlers were assigned to the rear to keep watch in case the enemy tried to flank them. After the battle, Liney again led the Marines safely back to their base.

Peppy

Doberman Peppy was stationed in Guam. During the heat of one battle his handler put him in a safe foxhole so that he would not be shot by the Japanese, who specifically targeted dogs. When, later, his handler looked to see if he was still there, the dog was nowhere to be seen, and searching for Peppy was out of the question. The handler suspected that he had been frightened and had run off. Three days later Peppy turned up: despite a bullet wound to his head, he had managed to return to duty. Peppy was an example of the courage and devotion such dogs displayed.

Marines and their Devil Dogs.

Coast Guard

The U.S. Coast Guard learned early in the war that dogs were a prime necessity. There were many places along the shores of the United States that were often entombed in dense fog. This was the case along a beach in Long Island in June 1942. It was during a dense fog that a German U-boat surfaced about 500 yards offshore. As a lone, unarmed Coast Guardsman, Second Class Seaman Cullen was patrolling his six-mile stretch when he encountered three men. Two were standing in water next to a dinghy and one was on the beach. When approached by Cullen, the man on the beach claimed they were fishermen who had run aground. As Cullen talked with the man, he realized they were German saboteurs, but pretended to believe their story. He then witnessed the men unloading some boxes and asked if they were clams, knowing that there were no clams in that area. The German said the boxes were indeed clams. After the exchange, Cullen was able to quickly return to the Coast Guard station and sound the alert. When they returned to the beach, the Germans were gone. However, the next day, members from the Coast Guard, Federal Bureau of Investigation, Army, and Navy found buried deep in the sand dunes boxes which contained bombs, fuses, timing devices, and detonators. These had been made to look like pen and pencil sets and pieces of coal of all things.

Mixed-breed Sinbad was enlisted into the Coast Guard in 1937 as a puppy so that he could stay on board the USS *Campbell*. While not trained as a military dog, he would serve throughout World War II on the ship, and did his bit for the war effort. His exploits on the *Campbell*, which was assigned to convoy escort duty in the Atlantic, were widely publicized, and he would appear in photo sessions and news interviews when the *Campbell* was in port to raise morale at home; photo-stories about him appeared in *Life* magazine twice during the war. (U.S. Coast Guard)

Attack training for a Coast Guard dog.

The Germans used the same tactic on other parts of the East Coast but were discovered. This led to the realization that dogs were the best means to patrol the beaches and to detect saboteurs in dense fog. Coast Guard sentry or patrol dogs were used in less-populated beach areas because the Coast Guard felt that the dogs should not be allowed to have contact with too many people. They felt it would desensitize the dogs to intruders. The Coast Guard also used mounted horseback patrols in more populated areas. Ultimately, the dogs patrolled the entire coastline of the United States as well as American assets in Newfoundland and Iceland. Dogs were also used at many of the Navy's shore installations.

Unlike the Marines, who preferred Dobermans and German Shepherds, the Coast Guard used all the breeds and mixed breeds that the Army used. However, they did prefer German Shepherds or German Shepherd crosses. One reason why they preferred this breed is because their size and coats provided protection for the dogs in the sometimes bitter weather in which they worked.

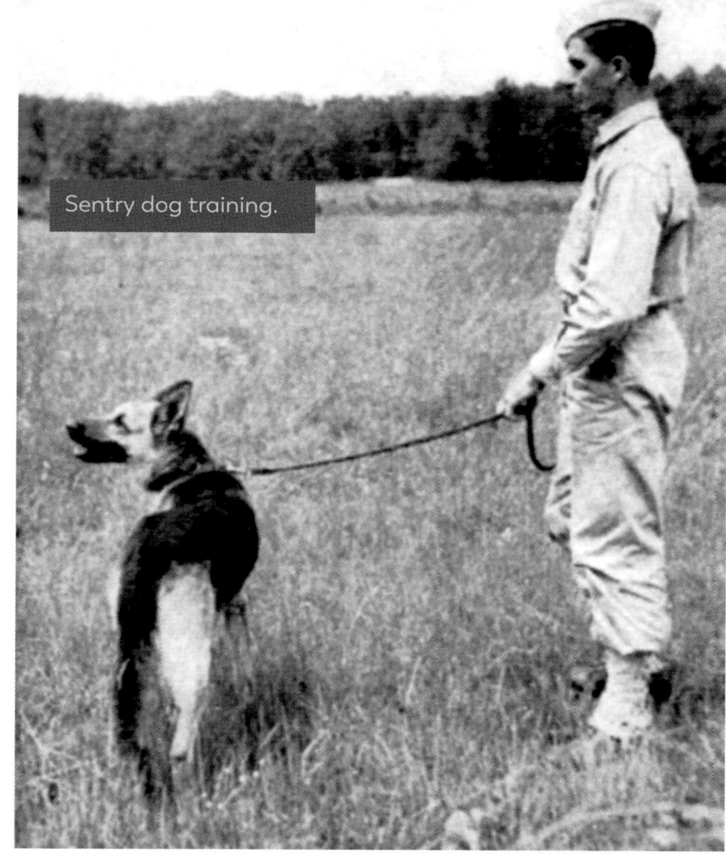

Sentry dog training.

Coast Guardsman and Gus, the son of the famous dog Chips of the Pacific.

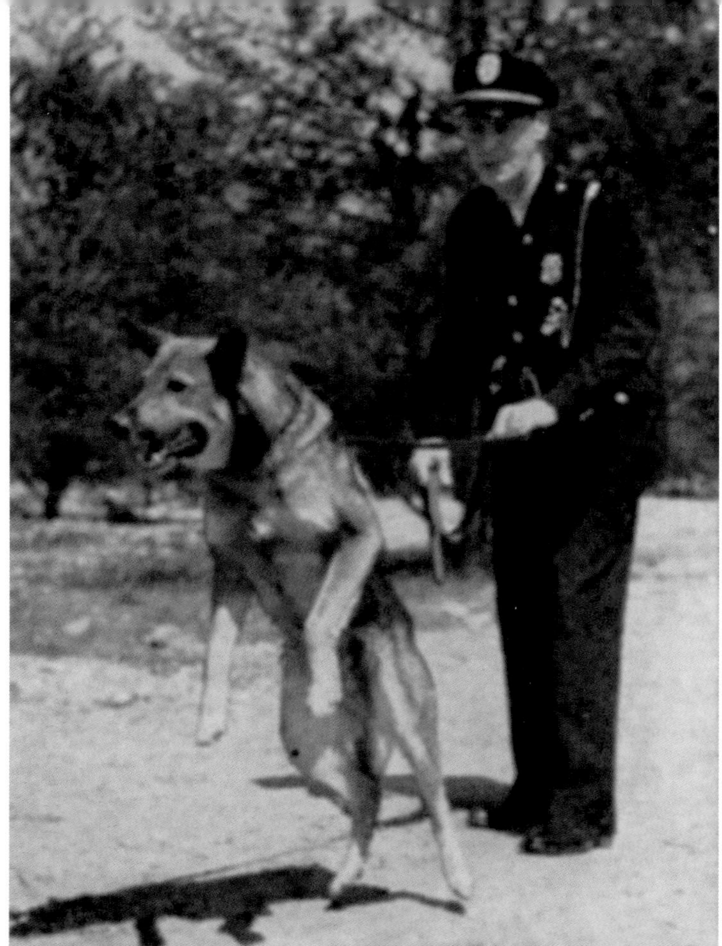

Sentry dog ready to attack.

Sentry dog on guard with his handler.

The use of patrol dogs in the Coast Guard was so effective that they were able to reduce the number of dogs by a fourth, allowing the trained dogs to be deployed elsewhere. Although most of the dogs were German Shepherds, there is an account of a Chesapeake Bay Retriever named Dipsy Doodle who became famous. A tanker had been torpedoed off the coast of New Jersey. Dipsy Doodle found the body of a seaman in the water and brought it to shore. Before the night set in, he recovered the bodies of 21 more seamen.

Coast Guard handlers were as devoted to their dogs as any soldier or Marine. Nora was a German Shepherd and the pet of Apprentice Seaman Mitchell, but she had been trained for patrol work. On a bitter winter's night, they were on patrol when Mitchell became sick and passed out. Nora immediately grabbed his cap and ran back to the Coast Guard station where she gave the cap to a chief boatswain's mate. Since the cap had Mitchell's name in it, the men were able to ascertain that it was Mitchell on duty. Nora was acting in a highly excitable state and led the men back to Mitchell, who was still lying unconscious on the beach where the high tide would soon have reached him. Nora had saved Mitchell's life and was later awarded a bronze John P. Haines Medal by the ASPCA.

Unnamed military dog.

Coast Guardsman and his sentry dog.

Coast Guardsman and dog watching the beach.

Some Outstanding Dogs

The following are accounts of individual dogs. Some records are scanty, giving little information about the dog and the incident, while others are more detailed. What is important is that the brief reports reflect that the handler or soldier who wrote the report felt that the dog was outstanding enough to be included. Even a brief account is important, as many World War II animal stories have been lost forever.

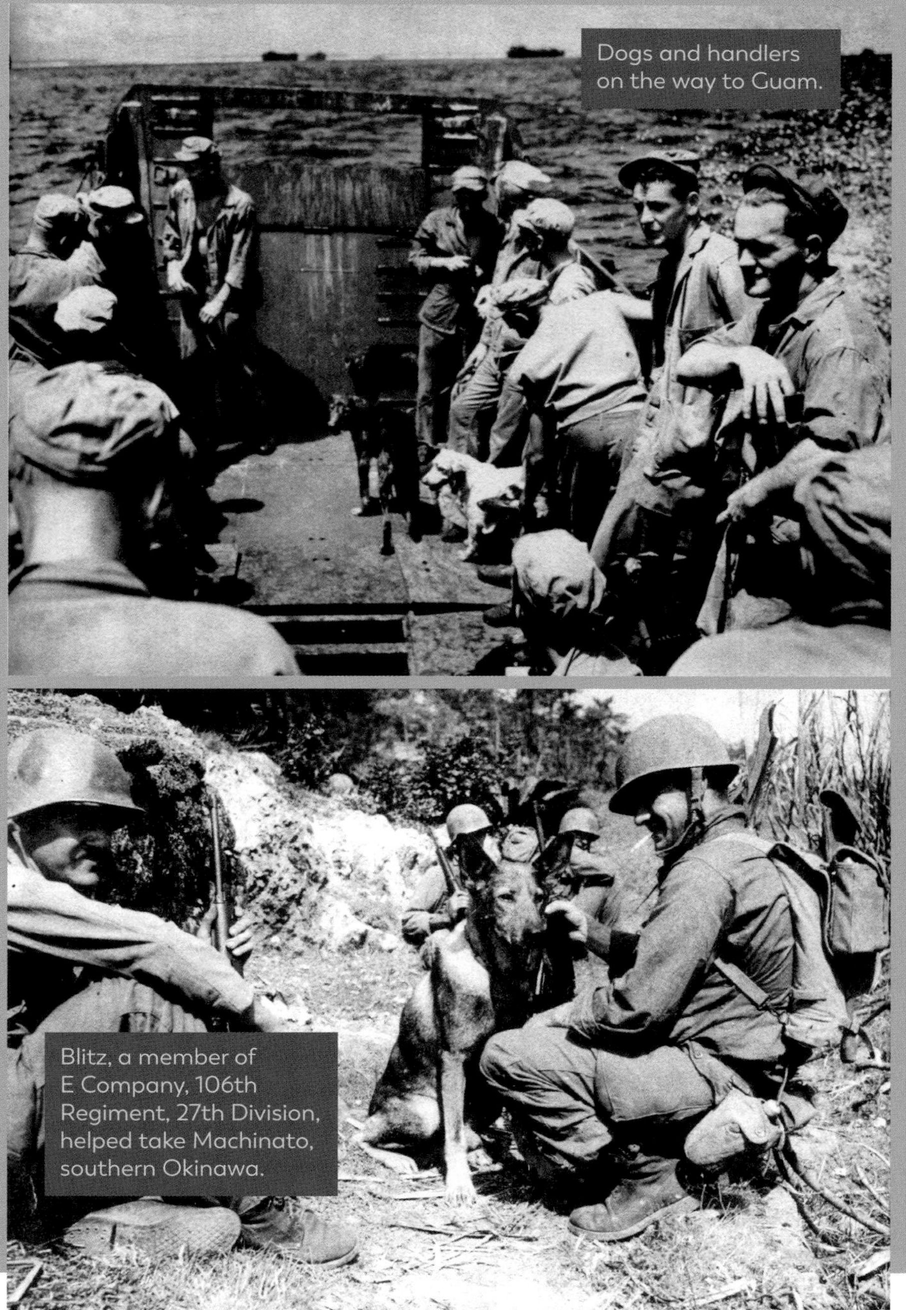

Dogs and handlers on the way to Guam.

Blitz, a member of E Company, 106th Regiment, 27th Division, helped take Machinato, southern Okinawa.

Dog Duke and his handler on a Pacific Island.

Rolf

Rolf and his handler were patrolling a Boston war plant when suddenly Rolf, a beefy Boxer, froze. His handler unclipped the leash from Rolf's collar and whispered "Find." Rolf quickly disappeared into the night. Within a few minutes, a scream was heard as Rolf attacked a saboteur. Rolf's handler ran toward the noise, grabbed Rolf by the collar and commanded him to "Off." He quickly handcuffed the man, who was whimpering in pain. Rolf stood next to his handler, ready to attack again if the saboteur moved the wrong way. When the police examined the man, they found a complete plan to destroy the factory. Had the saboteur succeeded, the people on the night shift would have been killed or injured and the plant put out of operation.

Danny and Jack

Danny and Jack, two German Shepherds, were stationed at the United States Army Air Force school at Stuttgart, Arkansas. One evening just after mess, Jack's handler was sitting in a field relaxing with Jack after a day of patrolling. Jack was rolling on the ground, scratching his back in the grass and waving his paws in the air, his favorite activity in the evening. Suddenly, Jack jumped up and lifted his nose to the breeze. His body froze as he pointed toward the guardhouse. His handler was surprised because Jack's alert was not the kind he would give for an intruder. Jack started to move toward the guardhouse in a stealthy manner, with his handler following. Then his handler saw it, a slight wisp of smoke coming out of the guardhouse. It was on fire. The soldier sounded the alarm, and the fire was put out before it could do much damage or harm anyone. Two days later, Danny was on patrol with his handler when he lowered his head and the hackles rose on his back. This was not the signal that he gave for a saboteur or a trespasser. He was pointing to the lumber yard. When Danny's handler investigated, he found that someone had started a small fire. He quickly put it out before the fire consumed valuable wood. After both fires were investigated, it was determined that they had been purposely set.

Rex

German Shepherd Rex had been assigned the number P-40. He was on patrol on an island in the South Pacific. All was quiet. The waves gently lapped at the shore and the birds seemed undisturbed. Rex never paid attention to the birds but suddenly his handler noticed that he was focused on a spot offshore where some gulls were swimming. Rex was tense and focused. Thinking that Rex was looking at the gulls, Rex's handler tried to calm Rex, but the dog started growling. A few minutes later, Rex's handler spotted a Japanese boat trying to land.

Butch

Iwo Jima was covered with sandy volcanic ash and rocks. Around February 1945, communications were out and the only way to send a message was by using Butch, a Belgian Shepherd Dog. The fighting had been fierce and the men needed urgent resupplying. Butch's handler put a message in a metal tube and fastened it to Butch's collar. He put his arm around the dog's neck and quietly whispered in his ear: "Boy, we are depending on you. Report!" Butch took off like a shot, heading for his other handler just over a mile away. Bullets zipped all around around him as Butch's handler prayed that he would make it. Within six minutes, Butch had delivered the message, unhurt.

Carl

"Hell's Island" is what the Japanese called Guadalcanal, an island in the South Pacific. It was a hellish place, but it had a single dirt airstrip that was strategically critical to both the Japanese and the Americans. Soldiers on both sides suffered from the jungle conditions, heat, humidity, lack of food, and disease. A group of Marines were posted there from August 1942 to February 1943. One night, they were trying to get some sleep between Japanese assaults. Carl the dog and his handler Ray were on guard duty in their forward foxhole. Because the Marines did not want to make a noise and give away their position, Ray had a unique way of quietly alerting the sleeping soldiers: he tied a string from his foxhole to the feet and hands of his fellow Marines in their nearby foxholes. By pulling on the string, he could quietly alert the soldiers to danger. One night, Ray saw Carl go to alert. Within a few seconds, he alerted twice more. Ray tugged on the string and the wakened Marines quickly manned their positions. A large force of Japanese soldiers was trying to sneak up on the sleeping Americans. Carl's early warning saved all their lives that night and only two Marines were wounded in the firefight, while several enemy troops were killed.

Barron

In World War II, arguably one of the roughest pieces of terrain that the Marines had to face was Motobu Peninsula on the north of the island of Okinawa. With deep, sharp ravines and high, narrow, heavily wooded ridges, it was almost impossible to detect the enemy. The Marines had worked their way to the Motobu Peninsula and as a result, most of the northern Japanese forces were cornered there. Doberman Pinscher Barron was leading an advance with his handler, Coats, when the dog gave a strong alert. Although the Marines couldn't see or hear anything, they took cover in a nearby abandoned trench. Almost immediately, the Japanese attacked. During the attack, while Coats was lying in the trench, Barron gave another alert. The handler then spotted a column of Japanese soldiers sneaking up a trail on the Marines' flank. The alerted Marines repelled the attack.

Dogs on the Home Front

James M. Austin owned Saddler, a world champion Fox Terrier whom he had purchased from a breeder in England. Austin used some of the money that Saddler had earned through stud fees, dog food ads, and soap ads to benefit the war effort: to help pay for a Spitfire, to help British Blitz victims and to help fund the RAF fighter benevolent fund. In the U.S. his donations went to the Red Cross, an infantile paralysis fund, Dogs for Defense, hospitals, and visiting nurses' associations, and Saddler became quite famous.

Austin then came up with an idea to raise money to help support the troops in the field. His idea was to sell honorary ranks and commissions for dogs that could not serve in the military for what he called the War Dog Fund. Dogs for Defense loved the idea and set up an office in New York City. The War Dog Fund offered military ranks, a certificate of rank, membership, a collar tag, and a window sticker as part of the fund-raising project. The program became so popular that in just over a year, 25,000 pets had contributed. Applications arrived from all over the world, including from soldiers, sailors, and Marines who also sent money to register their pets. There was another outcome that no one had foreseen. The status of dogs in the United States rose to an unprecedented high. The public, in general, gained a new respect and love for the 4-F (militarily unsuitable) dogs left behind.

A messenger dog getting instructions on Iwo Jima. Note the soldier pointing and the dog looking in that direction.

Marines and their dogs moving to the front on Iwo Jima.

Mascots

Mascots of all kinds were important to the men and women which they belonged to. They were so loved that soldiers and sailors would often risk their lives to save their mascots. Because of this, they are worthy of being included in this book.

The battle of the Coral Sea was over. The aircraft carrier *Lexington* had survived the battle, despite taking a hit from two torpedoes and at least two strikes from Japanese dive-bombers. She was traveling under her own steam, with things apparently under control, when a huge explosion rocked the ship. No one knows for sure what the cause was. It might have been gas fumes, but whatever caused it, it quickly became necessary to abandon ship. Rear Admiral Frederick C. Sherman was the captain and, in the scramble to see that his men got off the ship, forgot about Wags, his black Cocker Spaniel and constant companion for several years. When he remembered Wags, Sherman ran through the burning ship to the emergency cabin where Wags usually went. Wags was not there. Although it was difficult to breathe, Sherman continued his search until he found Wags in another section of the bridge. Sherman picked up the dog, hugging him close to his body, and handed him to an orderly. Only when the last man had left the ship did Sherman abandon it—and just in the nick of time, as the torpedo room exploded.

Men could sleep easy knowing that their dogs were with them.

Shipwreck, a little black and white nondescript dog, was the mascot of a Marine stationed in the South Pacific. Everyone loved Shipwreck and would laugh at his antics. For a brief period, Shipwreck would make the Marines forget about the war. He inspected their maneuvers, he was steady under fire, and was a great swimmer. Shipwreck guarded his owner's property and would not allow anyone near it. At night he had the special privilege of sleeping on his owner's bed.

General Eisenhower had a black Sottish Terrier named Telek who went everywhere with him, even to the Mediterranean Theater. Telek had been a gift from the British while Eisenhower was stationed in England, and he loved the little dog. When Eisenhower returned to England in preparation for the invasion of Western Europe, poor Telek had to go into a six-month quarantine as per British law. Despite his long working hours. Eisenhower managed to visit Telek at least once a week until his quarantine was over.

X, which stood for explosion, was a brown and white mixed-breed dog who was born during a huge explosion at Dutch Harbor on Kiska, an island in the Rat Islands group which is part of the Aleutian Islands of Alaska, a lonely, rocky outpost. His owner, Ensign Jones, had been posted there before the war to set up a radio station. Unfortunately, Jones was reassigned and his Navy buddies did not want X to leave, so Jones left X behind to keep them company. In June 1942, the Japanese captured the island and took the soldiers prisoner. The Japanese left X alone and he stayed with some local islanders. A little over a year later, the Japanese were forced to abandon the island and left X behind: an Allied amphibious force recaptured the island and were surprised when they were greeted by a party of one, a very happy X. The life of a mascot is not always easy.

Technical Sergeant Martin Metzler was a flight chief for an American bomber squadron whose mascot was a Scottie mix named Max. Somehow, Max knew when Metzler was going on a mission and refused to be left behind. As a result, Max had over 200 flying hours to his credit. When the airplane was above 10,000 feet, Metzler shared his oxygen mask with Max, who always remained calm.

Lieutenant-Colonel Harry G. Brady had a terrier mix named Mike. Brady was a paratrooper and had a special parachute and harness made up for Mike so that he could jump with him. Mike did not mind doing this and was credited with jumping from over 1,000 feet with the U.S. Sixth Army Air Corps. It is amazing what these "untrained" mascots could accomplish.

The story of Alma is not unusual. She was a stray who wandered into the hull of a merchant ship that was under construction. The workmen adopted her and she stayed with them in the steelyards. When a Navy gun crew took over the ship they adopted Alma, who sailed with them on convoy trips.

One fateful day, when Alma was taken ashore at a Pacific Coast port, she got separated from the sailor who had taken her to get her nails clipped. The ship put to sea that night and the crew was very upset that Alma was not with them. They were sure it was a bad omen. The story went public and a feature writer from the *New York World-Telegram* managed to find Alma. The ship was due to dock in New York and the writer arranged for Alma to be flown on a transport plane to meet the ship. However, before the ship arrived in New York, it was reassigned to North Africa. Poor Alma spent the next six months at the ASPCA waiting for her ship to come home. Finally, it did, and Alma and her gun crew had a very exciting and happy reunion.

The love servicemen had for their mascots has been illustrated more than once. They would risk their lives to save their canine companions. Such is the story of Queenie, a small mixed-breed dog. In a Mediterranean port, several Army transport ships were anchored next to each other near a group of oil tankers. With no warning, there was an explosion on one of the tankers. Smoke, fire, and oil shot out of the tanker, causing a huge oil slick which spread quickly over the water and could have caught fire at any moment. To avoid the danger, the transports put out to sea. In the rush to safety, Queenie, the mascot on one of the transports, fell overboard. Queenie struggled to stay afloat. Her coat was slick with oil. There were also heavy swells which made it difficult for her to swim. Corporal Clark spotted Queenie drowning, so he took off his clothes and jumped into the water to save the dog. The transports were a mere couple of feet from each other and Corporal Clark was in danger of being crushed. He reached Queenie, but the swells pulled her away. Time after time he tried to grab her. Finally, he caught her and was able to swim to the rope ladder that his shipmates had thrown over the side. Everyone cheered when he reached the deck with an oil-coated Queenie under his arm.

At three weeks of age, Skipper, a Collie mix, was taken aboard a Liberty ship by messman Paul Wolter. Skipper had only ever known life on board the ship and was happy. However, one fateful day in the Indian Ocean, the ship was torpedoed. The crew had to abandon ship. Wolter grabbed Skipper and handed him to a crewman, telling him to toss Skipper to him once he was in the ocean. Wolter caught Skipper as soon as the dog hit the water. His crewmate jumped in after them and they all swam to a life raft. Ten men and Skipper made it to the raft, but no one had any idea how long they would be afloat before being rescued. The men shared their rations with Skipper, one biscuit and three ounces of water a day, which they gave the dog in his master's shoe. For five days they drifted under the blistering sun. Finally, a British transport found them and took them to Cairo. The men felt that Skipper had brought them luck and kept their morale up.

A soldier had lost both his hands above the wrist and was deeply depressed, having lost the will to live. He would not look at what remained of his arms and would only speak when asked a question. One day, Chaplain Lieutenant-Colonel William E. King was making his rounds in the hospital tent. His tiny, 6-inch-long dog Lulabelle would often sit in his coat pocket. As King stood next to the soldier's bed, the soldier saw the dog peeking out of King's pocket and for the first time he spoke without being asked to. He asked the chaplain if he would let Lulabelle lick his face. King put Lulabelle on the soldier's bed, and she crawled up his chest and licked his face. The soldier explained that he had a dog at home and it would lick his face when he was sleeping. The soldier had tears in his eyes and a smile on his face. The chaplain left Lulabelle snuggled up in the soldier's armpit with her head on his shoulder. How much a mascot could mean to a soldier was sometimes the difference between wanting to live or not. Dogs were sometimes the only thing that represented home and normality for the men serving in war zones.

Corregidor is an island at the entrance to Manila Bay in the Philippines and was the site of intense fighting in World War II. Eventually, the U.S. Army recaptured the island but it was still being subjected to enemy air raids. One group of soldiers had a little black and white terrier named Subic. The sirens had gone off and a few minutes later the bombs began falling. Subic's squad had enough time to take cover, but Subic was still exposed. A bomb exploded near him and he was sent flying, severely wounded in one eye with his neck cut by shrapnel. Two soldiers saw what had happened and left the safety of their cover to save him. They picked him up, shaking and bleeding badly, and dashed without thinking amid the bombing and shrapnel to get Subic to the base veterinarian. Subic was operated on and his life was saved.

As difficult as it may seem, Sergeant Lloyd Worley and his comrades were able to smuggle Buster from the Army's Desert Training Center in California to North Africa. Buster was a stray who had wandered into the training center in California and won the hearts of the soldiers. Buster took it upon himself to protect the soldiers and their possessions from the native peddlers and thieves who tried to steal supplies. He also saved soldiers from harm by allowing soldiers to come and go at will but refusing to let anyone who wasn't a soldier come into camp. No one knows how Buster learned this.

More Courageous Dogs

Mena

Three other German Shepherds, Mena, Pal, and Watch, made the landing at Fedhala with Chips. The boat that Mena was in was hit by a shell just before landing. This caused Mena to suffer severe shell shock and she could not be used for patrol work. However, she bore a litter sired by Chips. When General Eisenhower learned about Mena's situation, he had her, her litter, and her caretaker, PFC Ewell N. McLester, returned to Front Royal. Because Chips had sired her litter, Mena was honored at the 1944 Westminster Dog Show in New York City.

King, on patrol at Aitape, New Guinea. Note the machine-gunner right behind King and his handler. The rest of the patrol is not visible.

The 26th War Dog Platoon in the jungle.

Pal

When Pal landed with Chips and Mena, his boat was shelled but it did not affect him as it had Mena. He was slightly injured but continued to patrol and guard at night. Pal and his handler, Corporal Ockman, patrolled the soldiers' bivouac areas. The sleeping troops needed to be protected from the enemy as well as locals. If a battalion did not have patrol dogs, the morning would find soldiers with their throats cut, and/or their clothing and equipment stolen.

Scout dog on patrol in the jungle.

Pal was also a courageous dog. In one battle when his battalion was pinned down by machine-gun fire, Ockman told Pal to "Get them!" Pal ran under the machine-gun fire, dove into the machine-gun nest, and attacked the enemy. He grabbed the gunner by the throat and ripped out his jugular vein. The other two soldiers in the nest jumped up to get away from Pal and in doing so, exposed themselves and were shot. Pal was so intense in his attack that Ockman had a hard time in getting him to release the enemy soldier's neck. Pal was awarded a Silver Star.

Sergeant Fleabite

It is hard to imagine a Pomeranian war dog, but Sergeant Fleabite was indeed a Pomeranian. Sergeant Fleabite "enlisted" with his master in the United States and stayed with him through training. They were transported to England on a troopship and from there they deployed to France on D-Day. Surviving D-Day, they were sent into battle at Saint-Lô where the unit came under heavy shellfire. Fleabite had been taught to dive into a foxhole or a slit trench when under bombardment. During the battle, Fleabite was lying next to his master when he detected the sound of an incoming shell. He quickly ran for a foxhole and his master and another soldier instantly followed him. When they looked back, they saw that an 88mm shell had exploded exactly where they had been.

Sergeant Fleabite's master received shrapnel wounds, though none of a serious nature. He was, however, sent to a hospital in England and thanks to Field Marshal Montgomery, he was not separated from Fleabite; they were allowed to return home together. Fleabite was awarded a special medal for saving his master's life.

Messenger dog waiting for the command to report.

Teddy

Teddy participated in the Cape Gloucester operation on the island of New Britain as part the wider New Guinea campaign. Teddy was assigned to the Sixth Army Marine Raider Regiment. The aim of the operation was to capture two Japanese airfields. Teddy's main jobs were as a patrol and messenger dog. Teddy saved the lives of many soldiers and was respected enough to be mentioned in reports.

Sandy

Sandy was an exceptionally devoted messenger dog. On one occasion he had to take a message from his handler back to the command post. On top of having to work his way through Kunai grass, a grass so tough and tall that it is used as roof thatching, Sandy had to swim across a river, and then crawl under mortar and tank fire. If that was not enough of an ordeal, he then had to negotiate barbed-wire obstacles. What makes this story even more incredible is that Sandy had not seen his handler, Sergeant Sheldon, since the previous night, and Sheldon had relocated some distance away. Nevertheless, Sandy still found him. Sandy's intelligence and bravery in completing his mission awed the soldiers who worked with him.

Wolf

Another dog who did not shirk his duties despite being wounded was Wolf. He was assigned to the 27th Infantry Division and was engaged in fighting in the Corabello Mountains in northern Luzon, the Philippines. The enemy was strongly entrenched in the area and Wolf alerted his patrol to their location. An intense firefight ensued. No one noticed that Wolf had been wounded by shrapnel. The patrol was obliged to withdraw to their base camp, with Wolf continuing to guard the patrol in silence. The patrol had vital information that it had to get back to headquarters. On the way back, Wolf alerted the patrol to

Hey, a German Shepherd and Chow mix.

enemy presence on three separate occasions. Back at base, Wolf's handler saw that he was wounded. Immediately, the dog received the best medical care, including surgery.

Hey

Hey was a German Shepherd sentry dog assigned to an area west of Henderson Field along the Matanikau River in Guadalcanal. Hey had a solid reputation as a nasty dog because en route to the South Pacific, he had bitten some two dozen soldiers who had tried to be befriend him.

Hey was leading a patrol on the beach with his handler when he froze. His handler noticed that Hey's ears were standing straight as he intently sniffed the air. Then a deep, menacing growl rumbled in his throat. In a heartbeat, Hey leaped across the rocks toward the beach. His handler and the other soldiers hit the dirt as a series of shots rang out and Hey dove into a clump of bushes. A disheveled figure jumped up and ran toward the beach with Hey in hot pursuit. Hey grabbed the Japanese soldier, but the sniper managed to break free and dove into the surf. Hey did not give up and grabbed the man again. The Japanese sniper surrendered. It wasn't long after that Hey was sent to Australia and then back to Hawaii for more training. He was finally deployed to the Southwest Pacific. The soldiers who worked with him noted that although he was small, he made up for it with his aggression and courage.

Bronco

Bronco, a Pointer, also served on Guadalcanal. The Marines had captured a Japanese flier and were holding him prisoner. When the Military Police Officer on duty made his rounds, he saw that the flier had escaped. He sounded the alarm, and right away Bronco's handler let him loose to track the flier. Bronco took off like a shot, hot on the man's trail. Out of the compound and down to the beach Bronco flew, the military police officers breathlessly behind him. On the beach, the officers saw the flier was trying to head toward the ocean to swim away, but he was caught and taken back into custody.

Great Britain and the Commonwealth

Even though there was no official war dog program in 1939, there were about 600 dogs working with the troops of the British Expeditionary Force (BEF) in Belgium, France, and North Africa. One of the more famous messenger dogs, a German Shepherd named Mark, was so loved that he was one of the 200 dogs evacuated from Dunkirk in 1940.

Mark, one of the dogs rescued at Dunkirk.

Because of the war, supplies of food were limited and at the beginning of 1940, rationing was instituted. Adults received a buff-colored booklet; green was designated for pregnant and nursing women, and families with children under 5 years of age; blue booklets were issued for children between the ages of 5 and 16. Because no one knew how long the war would last,

some cats followed the bases as they moved. These were dogs that had been abandoned by their masters or were survivors of bombing raids. Some had been made pets of soldiers who had shipped out. They became a problem and some even formed packs which attacked local flocks of sheep. As a result, the RSPCA and the People's Dispensary for Sick Animals (PDSA) were called into action. They realized that the dogs were being fed food that people needed, but that destroying the pets would not be accepted by the general population.

As the war continued, both the United States and the UK needed dogs to protect critical sites as Operation *Overlord* ramped up, and enemy saboteurs were on the rise. Colonel Baldwin, who ran the Guard Dog School, was called upon to provide these dogs, called Vulnerable Point Dogs. These dogs had been used with some success at the U.S. Army Air Forces bases in Northern Ireland, where eight dogs patrolled the aerodromes. The prime minister's residence, as well as the UK's entire civil and war-making infrastructure, were patrolled by dogs. As word of the dogs' success spread, by 1944 about 200 dogs a month were being requested. This resulted in another appeal to the British people to donate their dogs to the war dog effort, as well as any qualified strays.

Paradogs

Britain instituted a program to train paradogs to jump from airplanes with paratroopers. The program started because of a human-interest story about a dog named Tess. She was a German Shepherd who had been the mascot of the 190 Transit Camp Mediterranean Expeditionary Force (MEF) in Egypt and had been taught to jump with her master.

As a means of keeping the paratroopers in shape until D-Day, the Parachute Regiment decided to experiment in training dogs to jump. By 1942, the British had taught dogs to

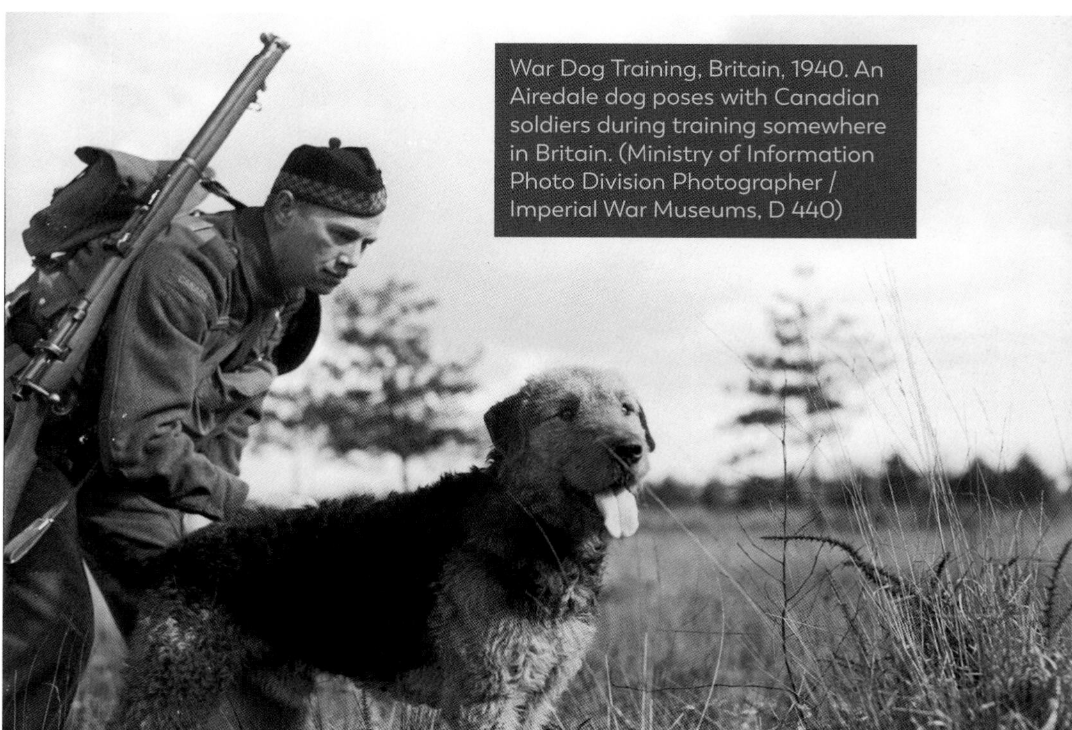

War Dog Training, Britain, 1940. An Airedale dog poses with Canadian soldiers during training somewhere in Britain. (Ministry of Information Photo Division Photographer / Imperial War Museums, D 440)

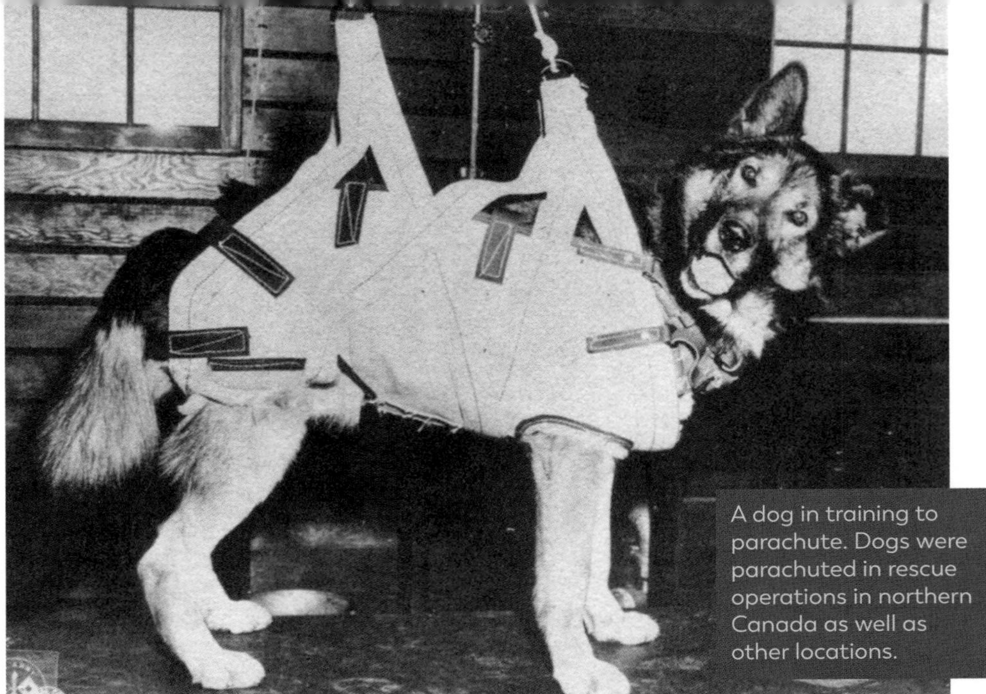

A dog in training to parachute. Dogs were parachuted in rescue operations in northern Canada as well as other locations.

parachute behind enemy lines. These dogs were not attached to a soldier's harness as they are today but parachuted next to them. Once on the ground, the dog would wait for his handler to find him to remove the parachute. Then the dog would lead the soldiers on patrol, giving a silent alert to any enemy presence. Although there is little information about a dog named Rob, he was reported as being exceptional. Rob was a black and white mixed breed who worked with the Special Air Service (SAS). He never failed to alert the soldiers to the presence of the enemy in North Africa and Italy. Rob made a dozen jumps into enemy territory.

On D-Day, the 13th Parachute Battalion was the main unit to jump with dogs. The Scout Platoon was divided into four groups of 10 men with three of the groups having one dog. Another dog, Glen, a German Shepherd, jumped with A Company, 9th Parachute Battalion. The objective of the drop was to clear and hold an area near Ranville, a French village. Ranville was the first village liberated on D-Day. From here, the paratroopers controlled access to the River Orne. The paratroopers were also ordered to clear a path for gliders to land. The landing zone had mines placed on top of poles to prevent the gliders from landing. It was not unusual for abandoned German dogs, or those whose handlers had been killed, to be taken in by the British soldiers. Some of the German dogs were retrained and served with the British, while some were kept as mascots.

Jaint de Notimoreney is the only dog to have jumped into combat with American paratroopers.

The Allied Forces Mascot Club

People, both military and civilian, loved their animals so much that in 1943, the People's Dispensary for Sick Animals (PDSA) formed a special club known as the Allied Forces Mascot Club which was limited to animals. Its first member was a donkey named Barney. He was only a baby when adopted by the Hendon Air Station, which was the headquarters of the Anglo-American Air Unit. The PDSA was formed early in the war. Its mission was to care for sick animals, and to rescue homeless pets and those injured in air raids. Many soldiers' mascots were brought to the PDSA. The Allied Forces Mascot Club recognized the important role that these animals (including birds) played during the war. Today we call them therapy animals, assistance animals, or service animals. Although their role did not include direct military work, they gave comfort to many soldiers and civilians alike. Some were important for the mental and physical recovery of wounded soldiers. Many of these animals, although not trained for military roles, went into battle and some were even killed in action.

Dinghy was born on the Isle of Mull and was known for being very entertaining. He could count and do numerous tricks. He was the mascot of the 422 Squadron.

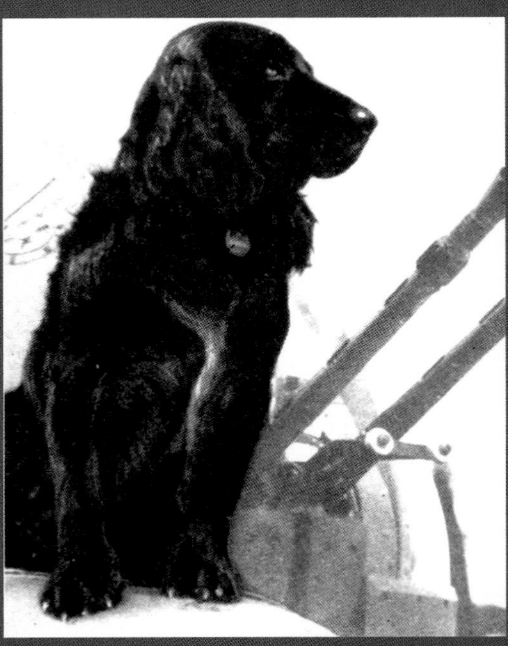

Straddle was the son of Dinghy and became the mascot of the 422 Squadron when Dinghy and his master were transferred.

The Dickin Gallantry Medal

The Dickin Gallantry Medal was created in the United Kingdom in 1943 by Maria Dickin to honor all animals who had provided outstanding service, gallantry, or devotion to duty in World War II. Maria Dickin was the founder of the People's Dispensary for Sick Animals (PDSA), the veterinary charity.

Bob

Bob was a superstar, patrolling and carrying messages. However, he earned his Dickin Gallantry Medal in March 1944 for one particular patrol. Bob was assigned to the Queen's Own Royal West Kents, an infantry outfit that was sent to infiltrate enemy lines at Green Hill in North Africa. Bob was the unit's messenger dog and at night, because Bob was mostly white, he had to be camouflaged. As the patrol worked their way into the enemy lines, Bob froze and gave a warning. The patrol leader waited, but as he didn't detect anything he decided to continue. Bob stayed frozen in place. He refused to move. It wasn't long before they detected enemy movement a few yards away. The patrol then safely withdrew to their lines with the knowledge of their enemy's whereabouts. Bob also took part in the Sicilian and Italian campaigns.

Bob, a patrol and messenger dog.

Rob

Rob, a cross-bred Collie, made over 20 parachute jumps in North Africa with the SAS, often into enemy territory. He was awarded the Dickin Gallantry Medal on January 22, 1945. Rob was born in Rannoch, Perthshire, in Scotland. When only a few months old, he was taken to England to work on a farm. He became the family pet and helped with the cattle, kept the chickens out of the garden, and helped the farmer's young son learn to walk by holding onto the dog's coat.

As food became scarce, the family donated Rob to the war effort to be trained as a paradog. Rob loved jumping out of airplanes. On command and without hesitation, he would leap into the air. Once on the ground, he would lie still until his handler came to remove his parachute. Rob served in Italy and once jumped with the paratroopers behind enemy lines, where they had

Rob the paradog made over twenty jumps.

Rob receives his medal for service.

to remain for months. Rob kept guard and protected the paratroopers until they were able to return home. Once in England, he accompanied a group of paratroopers to London to raise money for the Returned British Prisoners of War Fund. After his fundraising stint, he returned to military duty until 1945. After the war, he was returned to his family, and his farm duties, as if he had only been gone three hours and not three years.

Bing

Bing, a German Shepherd–Collie cross, parachuted into Normandy with the 13th Parachute Battalion, 6th Airborne Division. He was awarded the Dickin Gallantry Medal on March 29, 1947. Bing's original name was Brian. Because of rationing, his family, the Fetches, who lived in Loughborough in Leicestershire, could not feed him so they donated him to the British War Dog Program. He was sent to the Army War Dog Training School near Potters Bar in Hertfordshire. He

Bing, a German Shepherd–Collie cross, parachuted into Normandy.

was handled and trained by Lance-Corporal Ken Baily of the 13th Parachute Battalion. During the drop over Normandy on D-Day, he landed in a tree and had to be rescued. He was later wounded in action. He served in France until September 1944, when he was reassigned to a new handler, Corporal Jack Walton, and served in Operation *Varsity* and Operation *Plunder* before the advance into Germany. After the war, he was returned to the Fetch family and lived until 1955.

Antis

Antis, a German Shepherd, served with Václav Robert Bozdêch, a Czech airman who served in the French Air Force and in No. 311 (Czechoslovak) Squadron, RAF. Antis helped his master escape after the death of Jan Masaryk, the Czech diplomat and politician. Antis was the only dog who was allowed to fly on combat missions, with the aircraft often hit by antiaircraft fire during bombing raids. Antis was awarded the Dickin Gallantry Medal on January 28, 1949.

It all began when Bozdêch, a gunner, was flying a reconnaissance mission over Germany with his pilot, Duval, when they were shot down and crash-landed in no man's land between France and Germany. Duval was wounded but Bozdêch was not, so Bozdêch dragged Duval to an abandoned farmhouse. When they entered the farmhouse, a small German Shepherd puppy, emaciated and weak, crawled over to them. Bozdêch melted some snow for water and gave the puppy some of his rations. When night came the men left the puppy in the house, but the puppy started howling. Bozdêch went back and put the puppy in his jacket so that he would not attract the attention of the Germans, who were looking for downed pilots. They made it back to the French lines and the puppy—soon named Antis—bonded with the airmen, especially Bozdêch.

It wasn't long before the men realized that Antis would alert by standing stiff-legged, hackles raised, and growling long before anyone could see or hear the Luftwaffe Dornier Do 17 bombers approaching. Antis became an early warning system for the men. Later, Bozdêch was transferred to Liverpool, England. As he and Antis were walking one evening, Antis gave his alert and shortly enemy planes began bombing the city. Bozdêch and Antis were uninjured but right after the raid, Antis started sniffing the rubble and located six survivors, including a baby who had been trapped in the debris.

Bozdêch was then reassigned to an airbase in Suffolk, but Antis was not allowed to fly with him. When Bozdêch went on a mission, Antis would refuse to eat, sleep, or interact with anyone until Bozdêch returned. One day, with 20 minutes left before takeoff, Bozdêch was unable to find Antis anywhere. He then had to head to his bomber and take off. It wasn't until he was in the air that Bozdêch discovered that Antis had hidden himself in the bomber. When they reached cruising altitude, Bozdêch shared his oxygen mask with Antis so that he could breathe. Although it was strictly forbidden for a dog to fly on missions, officers later made an exception for Antis, who even got his own specially designed breathing apparatus. Even though Antis was twice wounded in action, he flew with Bozdêch rather than getting left behind.

Antis's adventures did not end when the war ended. When Bozdêch returned to Czechoslovakia, he took Antis with him. However, when the communists took over the country, Bozdêch had to flee with Antis to get back to Britain. Antis helped Bozdêch escape Czechoslovakia undetected by alerting him to border patrols en route. Once in England, Antis lived a peaceful life and reached the age of 13. Bozdêch loved Antis so much that he never owned another dog.

Tish

Tish, a mongrel, was found at El Alamein during the Western Desert Campaign and showed exceptional courage and devotion while serving with the 1st Battalion, King's Royal Rifle Corps. Tish was an excellent alarm for incoming shells. She was awarded the Dickin Gallantry Medal on July 1, 1949. She was owned by Rifleman Thomas Walker and accompanied him at the front, usually riding on the hood of a Jeep or a Bren Gun Carrier. Walker was a medic and took Tish wherever he went. Lieutenant-Colonel E. A. W. Williams recommended Tish for the Dickin Gallantry Medal because of the courage and devotion that she had shown during battle. He credited her with setting an example for the men during dangerous times. She refused to leave her station on vehicles transporting wounded troops, often in the middle of battle. She served in North Africa and Italy and after the war, she helped raise money for the PDSA.

Rifleman Khan.

Khan

Khan, also known as Rifleman Khan, was a German Shepherd. He had worked as a patrol dog in 1942 and was assigned with his handler, Muldoon, to the 6th Cameronians, Scottish Rifles. In late 1943, he was reassigned as a mountain warfare dog with the 52nd Infantry Division and deployed to France in 1944. At night, during the battle of Walcheren Causeway in the Scheldt, Netherlands, shellfire hit the division's assault craft and it capsized. Khan swam ashore and then looked around for Muldoon, who did not know how to swim. Despite the shelling and the noise of battle, Khan heard Muldoon's cries for help and immediately jumped back into the water, swam out to Muldoon, and grabbed hold of his collar, pulling his handler to shore in the freezing water. He was awarded the Dickin Gallantry Medal on March 27, 1945.

Peggy, Peter, Prince, Smiler, and Texas

Peggy, a mix of German Shepherd, Airedale, and Black and Tan Hound, along with three Black Labradors, Peter, Prince, and Smiler, were mine-detection dogs working during the Dutch *Hongerwinter* ('hunger winter') of 1944/5, one of the severest winters that had struck the Netherlands in years. To add to the misery, bombing had broken the dike and flooded the town of Middleburg on the island of Walcheren.

On March 24, 1945, Operation *Plunder* was initiated, with the objective of crossing the Rhine. The mission was launched by the 21st Army Group under Field Marshal Bernard Montgomery. The dogs of the 4th Platoon were part of the mine-breaching assault. At about 1100 hours, the dogs were ferried across the river to clear mines in the villages of Rees and Groin. At the same time, the 51st Highland Division was fighting house to house. The unit's veterinary sergeant and driver were wounded within a few minutes of landing on the German bank. However, the dogs continued to work. One of the dogs noted for his exceptional performance was a Golden Labrador from Sussex, named Texas. He worked under continuous gunfire, shelling, and mortar fire and was able to clear the approaches to the bridge on both banks of the Rhine.

The dogs then cleared the railroad tracks so that supplies could be sent to the starving residents of the villages. There were several types of mines that the dogs had to find: the S-mine, which sent up a lethal wall of shrapnel waist high; the antipersonnel Schu-mine 42, which was a wooden box of explosives designed to blow a soldier's foot off; and lastly, the Teller mine, which was designed to blow up a tank. The problem was that mine detectors did not work in the area because of the nearby railroad tracks, which were picked up by the mine detectors as mines. So, it was up to the mine-detector dogs to find the mines. Two dogs, one on either side of the track, worked to do so and two dogs followed them to ensure that the lead dogs did not miss anything. If a dog found a mine, he would freeze or sit, and then the handler would mark the spot so the engineers could come and disarm the mine.

Monty and Peggy

Two German Shepherds, Monty and Peggy, were born in the British Army. When they were old enough, they were trained as mine-detection dogs. During training, their handlers realized that both dogs had an uncanny ability to detect the wooden "shoe mine" (Schu-mine 42). The dogs would point or freeze until the handlers disabled the mine. Once their training was completed, they were sent to France where they detected a vast number of these mines. Both dogs saved many lives during their service with the British Army.

Ricky

Ricky was a Welsh sheepdog donated by Mrs F. Litchfield of Bromley, Kent, and was trained as a mine-detection dog. He was assigned to clear the edges of the canal in Nederweent, Holland in December 1944. He was credited with finding all the mines in the area, except one. That mine killed the section commander and wounded Ricky in the head. Despite his wound, Ricky kept on working. Because he kept calm while working, no further mines exploded and no more soldiers were killed, even though they were operating as close as three feet from Ricky. This was an especially dangerous job because they were clearing a minefield, not just looking for random mines. Later, Ricky was used to find Schu-mines. Ricky was then returned to his owner, even though the authorities offered Mrs Litchfield as much as they were allowed to in order to keep him in the military. He was awarded the Dickin Gallantry Medal in March 1947.

Judy

Eight German Shepherds guarded the de Havilland Aircraft Factory in Hatfield, Hertfordshire. One was a dog named Judy. The following incident illustrates how attached the dogs were to their handlers. Judy had been assigned to Leading Aircraftman H. R. Smith. After they had worked together for about 18 months, Smith became sick and was admitted to hospital. Judy was assigned to another handler until Smith recovered. During one patrol, Judy and her temporary handler stopped by the sickbay to briefly see the orderly. After only a minute, Judy was taken back to her kennel and tied up for the night. Several hours later, the sickbay orderly called the dog compound to complain of a "wild" dog at the hospital. Miraculously, Judy had managed to slip her collar and had pawed at the dog compound gate until she got it open. She then found her way into the hospital, jumped over two beds, and landed on Smith's bed. Over the next 24 hours she managed to repeat her escape four times. No one could figure out how she knew Smith was in that sickbay. She had only stopped for a minute outside the building that one time.

Sheila

Sheila's story is unusual because she was the only dog to win the Dickin Gallantry Medal who was not a military or Civil Defence dog. She was a Farm Collie who helped manage livestock in the Cheviot Hills. During a blizzard in December 1944, an American Eight Air Force Flying Fortress crashed. Local shepherds, including John Dagg and his Collie Sheila, heard the crash. Despite the severe storm, which had reduced visibility to almost zero, they started out to find the airplane and any survivors. As they searched through the storm in the hilly terrain, Sheila stayed by her master's side. When they reached the top of a hill, Sheila indicated that something was ahead and, in an instant, ran out into the storm and disappeared. She had found the airmen who had survived the crash in a ravine trying to see out the storm. When the airmen spotted Sheila, they shouted as loud as they could. Dagg heard the men and called Sheila back to him to lead him to the airmen.

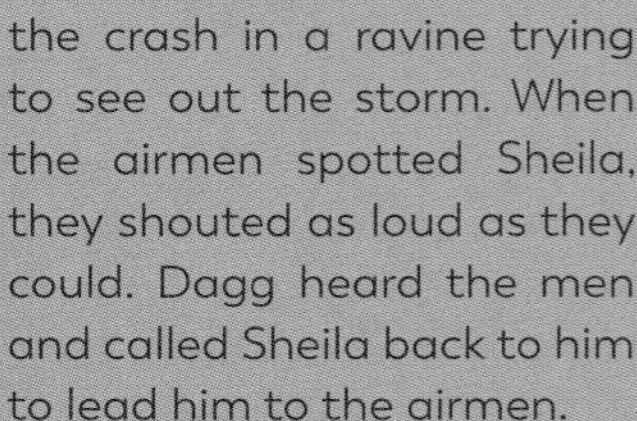

The story does not end there. The parents of one of the airmen who died in the crash had learned about Sheila and written to the War Department in Washington D.C. asking if they could obtain one of Sheila's puppies. After much red tape, their request was granted, and in July 1946, Tibby, a gorgeous white puppy, was sent to South Carolina. Sheila was awarded the medal in July 1945.

Sheila, a Border Collie who saved downed fliers.

Civil Defence Dogs

Although they were not military dogs, the Civil Defence Service (Air Raid Precautions, or ARP, until 1941) used dogs in the cities of Britain to find people trapped or buried in rubble and bombed-out buildings. At first, the dogs were an experiment to see if they would work, and were often handled by women issued with Civil Defence uniforms. The dogs had to find many blown-up and shattered body parts. For example, a workers' canteen in Erith took a direct hit from a rocket. The bodies were so fragmented that no one could tell how many people had been in the canteen. Even when targeted sites contained livestock, the dogs were not distracted; they worked well and stayed calm.

When bombing started in London, the PDSA formed squads that worked with the Civil Defence. They searched empty or destroyed buildings to help any surviving animals. Often pets wandered off, dazed, confused, and sometimes hurt, looking for their homes or owners. The squads would then treat any injured animals. They destroyed those who were beyond help. Civil Defence workers had to focus on those people injured or trapped and could not take care of animals. The animal rescue squads provided comfort to people who had lost everything by reuniting them with their pets.

Beauty, a Wirehaired Terrier, helped locate buried air-raid victims with the PDSA Rescue Squad. She was given an award on January 12, 1945. Beauty belonged to Bill Barnet, a PDSA veterinary officer who led one of the rescue squads. Beauty was instrumental in pioneering the use of dogs to find pets trapped in wrecked buildings and was considered the first true search-and-rescue dog.

At first, Beauty went with Barnet on rescue missions simply for company. Then one day, while on a mission with Barnet, she started to dig in the debris and found a cat. She had not been trained to do this but took it upon herself. She is credited with saving 63 animals trapped in bombed-out buildings.

Jet was a purebred German Shepherd from the Lada Kennels who had been trained as an anti-sabotage dog at the War Dog School in Gloucester at 9 months of age. When he finished his training, he was assigned to the troops in Northern Ireland where he worked for 18 months at airfields. After that assignment, he was sent back to school to become a search-

Beauty the Wire-Haired Terrier, Civil Defence dog.

Beauty the Civil Defence dog working the rubble pile.

and-rescue dog. He was then sent to London where he became the first dog to serve in the Civil Defence during the Blitz. He worked every night and is credited with finding 150 people in bombed-out buildings. His most famous rescue was at a hotel which had taken a direct hit. The rescue workers thought that they had gotten everyone out, but Jet had given a live-person alert and stayed on point for over 11 hours until a woman was pulled out from the upper floors. If that wasn't enough to validate Jet's service, after World War II he continued his rescue work during a mine disaster at the William Pit near Whitehaven, Cumbria, where he saved many miners. Unfortunately, he had breathed in gas in the mine and it affected his health. Jet died at 7 years of age and was buried at Calderstones Park by the Liverpool City Council.

Chum was a 12-year-old Airedale who had happened along at the right time. Chum was walking past a house that had been bombed in the Blitz when he heard a woman cry for help. Without any special training, he then tunneled through the debris to the woman. By doing this he allowed fresh air to reach her: she would have died due to a

Jet and Thorn, two Civil Defence dogs who saved many lives.

Thorn.

gas leak from a broken gas main. He stayed with the woman until the rescue crews could dig her out. Once the woman was freed, he left the scene.

In many cases after bombs had exploded, buildings and debris caught on fire. In one such instance, a street in West Ham was consumed in flames and Jet, a rescue dog on the scene, would not go through the smoke, but Thorn, another rescue dog, went through the thickest of the smoke and fire. Despite the intense heat, he gave an alert in the rubble. The rescue personnel scrambled to the spot and dug down, recovering the body of a fire victim. Thorn went on to search for more victims despite his burned paws and the intense heat and smoke.

During the Blitz, rescue workers used experimental, metal-cone sound-location devices to locate people in rubble, and felt that these were better than rescue dogs. This belief was proved wrong during one incident, where Mrs Griffin and four of her dogs, Irma, Bruce, Psyche, and Dawkin, were on site. The sound men had come onto the rubble, taken over the search, and dismissed the dogs. The sound device did detect people in the rubble but the rescuers lost their location. However, the dogs were able to pinpoint the missing people. They were so successful that more dogs were sent for training and the animals regained their status as search dogs.

Irma, a Civil Defence Dog.

Psyche, a Civil Defence Dog.

Irma had a special bark when someone was buried alive. On one rescue mission, she gave her live-find bark and did not leave the site for the two days it took the rescue personnel to dig down through the rubble, where they found two girls alive.

When on another mission Irma gave her alert, the rescue workers stopped and listened. Very faintly, they had heard a cry for help. It turned out that there were two sisters in a Morrison shelter. A Morrison shelter was a metal cage used during the war that allowed people to sleep in their homes. The purpose of the shelter was to protect people from falling debris. The rescuers were able to dig the sisters out. Unfortunately, one had been killed.

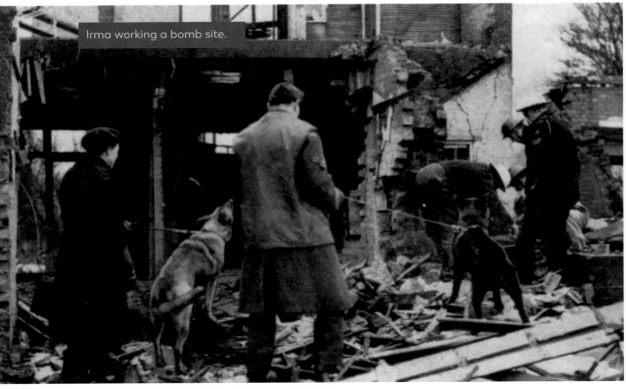

Irma working a bomb site.

In some cases, the dogs would find pets as well as people. In one instance, Psyche had found a cat but Irma kept giving her human alert. Digging further down, the rescuers found three bodies in the rubble.

Early one morning, Germany fired one of the last V-2 rockets that they would launch from Holland. It hit a working-class section of London. It leveled the terraced houses at Hughes Mansions on Vallance Road, Stepney, East London. The damage was devastating:

Rip at the site of a bombing.

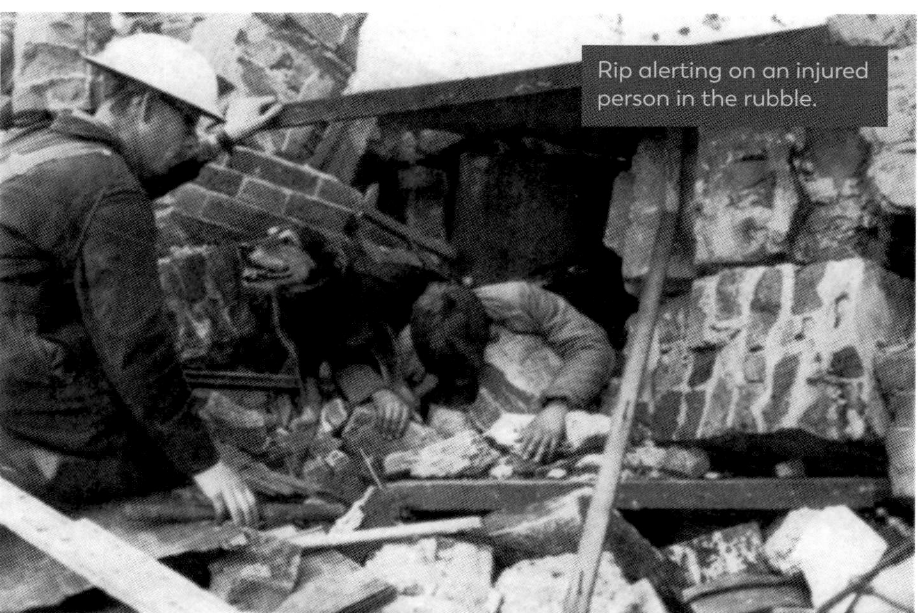

Rip alerting on an injured person in the rubble.

134 people were killed and 49 seriously injured. Peter and Rascal, who had been in training, worked the site. Peter, a 4-year-old Collie cross, worked for two hours but became exhausted. His lack of energy was due to the dogs only having been fed spoiled food, and even that was scarce. It took him a day to recover. He was a small dog but reported to work with real heart.

Rip, a large black dog, had been found hungry and homeless, and was adopted by a member of the rescue squad that worked in the East End of London. The area had been especially hard hit by the Germans because it was located near the docks. In one attack, a V-1 rocket hit a section of terraced houses with deadly results. The rescue squad, including Rip, rushed to the scene. Immediately, despite the hot, burning debris, Rip located a man buried deep in the rubble. Rip had not been formally trained to find missing people: he just did it on his own. Rip was later awarded a bronze medal for his gallantry throughout the war by Our Dumb Friends' League.

Jock was an Airedale Terrier whose home was destroyed by a bomb. Despite his wounds, Jock stayed all night at the wrecked house trying to dig through the debris to where his family was buried. His paws were sore and bleeding when the firemen came, but Jock refused to leave the rubble. The firemen dug down and found Jock's owner alive. Since his owner had no place to keep Jock, the firemen adopted him, but later, much to their regret, Jock's owner was able to take him back.

Rex, who had been in training, was being led over a well-worn path through the debris of some bombed-out buildings but then refused to go any further, and started to scratch at the wet, soft ground. When rescue workers dug down, they found blood and assumed it was from a previous incident of someone having been wounded. They tried to continue down the path, but Rex refused to leave. Trusting Rex, the men then dug down again and found the corner of some bedding which Rex tried to drag away. The rescue workers found bodies where Rex indicated they would be.

On another occasion, Rex worked tirelessly at a burning factory. The fire had been brought under control, and the debris was still hot, with fire hoses spraying water over the area. Rex found five people within his first four minutes of work. He continued to work other incidents as a rescue dog, despite being affected by gas.

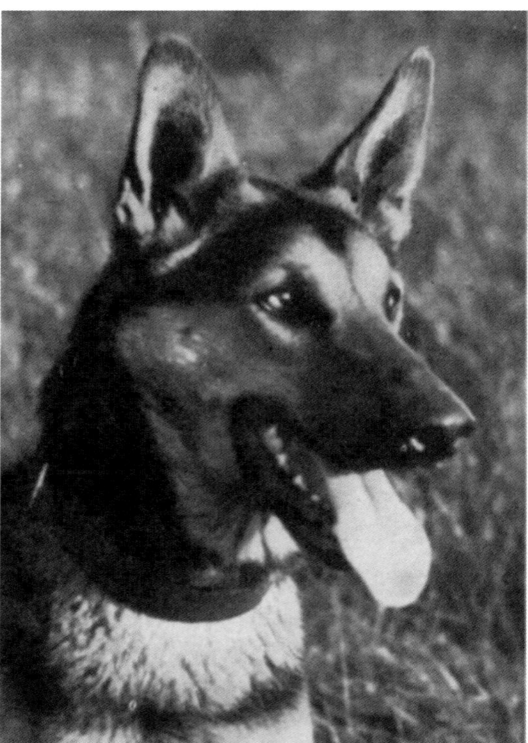

Rex, a very brave Civil Defence dog.

Heroic Civilian Dogs in Wartime

Fluff

Fluff was a family pet and although there is no record of her breed, it was noted that she was a small dog. Her home had been bombed during the Blitz and Fluff had managed to wiggle out of the rubble. However, she did not run away, hide, or otherwise cower in fear. She went back to the pile of rubble that had been her home and barked relentlessly, digging and scratching until the rescue personnel came and rescued her family.

Peggy

At times, the rubble and debris shifted as it settled, making it difficult to hear cries for help. Rescue personnel encountered pets who had not given up trying to dig their families out of the debris and sometimes even a stray gave an alert to buried people. Peggy, a 5-year-old Wirehaired Fox Terrier, was one of those untrained dogs whose love of people saved a mother and child who had been buried in their home. She scratched at the debris until rescuers saved the family.

Peg-Leg

Peg-Leg was a German Shepherd who had lived on the Isle of Man in the Irish Sea. Peg-Leg was so named because when he was a puppy, he had lost a leg. When Peg-Leg was 11 years old, he earned his claim to fame. An RAF aircraft had been flying from Horton Park Airport to the Isle of Man when it crashed into the side of Slieu Ruy, a peak on the island. There were five airmen on board. Three were killed instantly, one was trapped inside and badly injured, and the fifth was thrown free of the airplane. The latter airman had sustained broken ribs and a badly injured leg. Despite his injuries, he pulled himself over rough ground to get help, but after about a day and a half of crawling, he passed out. No one knew at the time how, but Peg-Leg found the man and instantly ran home to get help as fast as an old three-legged dog possibly could. When he reached his house, he ran up to his owner, barking, and tried to get him to follow. Peg-Leg was so insistent that his owner decided to see what the fuss was about. This behavior was something that he had never seen before in his dog. What a shock the man had when he found the wounded airman. He immediately gave the airman first aid and did the best he could for him. He then went for help. Because of Peg-Leg, the airman survived to fly another day.

Prince

Often people risked their lives to save their pets; equally, there are many accounts of dogs trying to rescue their owners from bombed-out buildings. Prince, a terrier, belonged to a 9-year-old boy named Harry. They were inseparable. Harry took complete care of Prince from feeding to grooming.

Prince saved his young master, Harry.

One night, Harry's family was asleep and no one heard the sirens. A bomb hit the house. Harry's parents were buried under beams, his grandfather was knocked unconscious, and Prince, crushed and blinded by plaster dust, was staggering around. Harry was buried in the rubble and had difficulty breathing because of the dust. Prince crawled to the area where Harry was buried and for almost an hour, dug, bit, and scratched until he managed to tunnel through to Harry, which allowed fresh air to reach the boy. Prince then reached through the tunnel and grabbed Harry's clothing to pull him out, but being unable to do so, he laid down next to the tunnel. He gasped for breath and barked until rescue personnel came and dug Harry out.

Eskimo dogs pulling sleds at Vesle Skaugum, a Norwegian training camp in Canada, January 1942. (IMS Vintage Photos {PD-US-expired})

Mascots

There are many interesting stories about mascots that illustrate how important they were to servicemen and women. Mascots were considered so important that at a conference of naval chaplains, it was decided to encourage ships to have mascots. They had noticed that when a seaman became agitated, unhappy, or depressed, the presence of a cat or dog worked miracles. Here are a few of the more famous mascots.

Judy, a purebred Pointer, was born in Shanghai in 1937 and was given to the Royal Navy as a mascot. Her adventures started while serving on HMS *Gnat* when she fell overboard into the Yangtze River; fortunately, she was rescued. After that she served on several different gunboats, and by 1942 was the mascot on HMS *Grasshopper*. During the Malay–Singapore campaign, HMS *Grasshopper* was attacked by Japanese dive-bombers. It caught fire and blew up. The surviving crew clung to some wreckage and followed Judy to the shore of an uninhabited island. The crew had not been able to save much food and did not find fresh water on the island. They were consumed with thirst and desperately searched the island for water. They left Judy behind on their searches so that she would not get even thirstier. Eventually, they took Judy with them. As they walked along a beach, they noticed that Judy kept hanging around around a particular area of the shore. When the tide went out, Judy went directly to the spot and started to drink: it was a freshwater spring.

Soon after that the crew managed to commandeer a Chinese junk. They then traveled to Sumatra, and from there hitchhiked to Padang where they were taken prisoner by the

Wing Commander J. E. "Johnnie" Johnson, commanding No. 144 (Canadian) Wing, on the wing of his Supermarine Spitfire Mk IX with his Labrador retriever, Sally, at Bazenville, Normandy, July 31, 1944. (PO Saidman RAF / Imperial War Museums, CL 604)

Japanese. All of them, including Judy, were held in a POW camp at Medan. During her imprisonment, Judy adopted Aircraftman Frank Williams of the RAF, who shared his daily portion of rice with her. Williams was able to convince the Japanese camp commandant, who was drunk at the time, to register Judy as an official POW, which gave her more protection and undoubtedly saved Judy's life. While in the jungle camp, Judy saved the lives of many prisoners, alerting them to poisonous snakes, scorpions, and even alligators and tigers. She also entertained the prisoners by chasing monkeys and flying foxes. They were thoroughly amused when she found the shinbone of an elephant and spent two hours digging a hole to bury it.

The Japanese then informed Williams that Judy was to be left behind as the POWs were to be transported by ship to Singapore. Williams would not hear it, so he stuffed Judy into a rice sack where she kept quiet for three hours, upside down. What had made it even more amazing was that Williams had to stand in the hot sun for two of those hours. The Korean guards watching the prisoners had been told to look out for Judy, knowing that the prisoners would try to sneak her on board the ship.

Once on the ship and out of sight of the guards, Judy was released from the sack for a much-needed break. Things remained quiet until the next day when the ship was hit by a torpedo. The men were trapped in the dark as the ship keeled over, but Williams noticed a small porthole that was too small for a man to crawl through but big enough for Judy, so he pushed her through. As soon as Judy was clear of the ship, another torpedo hit the ship, which somehow freed the prisoners who were then able to escape. After two hours the prisoners had all been picked up by the Japanese, but Judy was not among them. The men mourned, thinking that Judy had been killed by the Japanese or had drowned. But after three days, Judy miraculously showed up at the new POW camp. Unfortunately, the POW camp was run by the same commandant who had been at Medan and when he saw Judy, he was outraged. He ordered her to be killed and the prisoners to eat her remains. Carefully, the men found a hiding place for her and before the Japanese had time to find her, the war ended.

But Judy's adventures were not over. Judy and the POWs were freed by the British and put onto a troopship. Afraid that Judy would not be allowed to stay with him officially, Williams smuggled her onto the ship and managed to get her to England where she had to spend six months in quarantine, after which she was reunited with Williams. Judy lived to be 14. She was awarded the Dickin Gallantry Medal in May 1946.

Punch and Judy were a sibling pair of Boxers who saved two British

Judy, a famous prisoner of war.

Bacchus served in the RAF with his master, Flight Lieutenant C. H. Gardner, until the end of the war. Bacchus did not mind the sound of bombs or guns. He was noted for greeting new personnel and making them feel at home.

officers in Palestine by attacking a nationalist. They were awarded the Dickin Gallantry Medal in November 1946, just after World War II. In August 1946, the two officers were in their quarters with Punch and Judy. Because it was hot, the front door was open to catch any breeze that might provide some relief. As both men got up to check the area around their quarters before closing up and going to bed, both dogs jumped up and rushed outside into the garden. There was a burst of machine-gun fire and a yelp from one of the dogs. Terrorists had been waiting for the officers to come to the door to kill them.

When the police arrived, they followed a blood trail and found Punch laying in a pool of blood, dying, with Judy standing by his side. They immediately called the PDSA Superintendent of the Dispensary in Jerusalem. Despite the danger, the superintendent, traveled as quickly as he could to the location to try to save Punch. Upon examination, the superintendent found that Punch had four wounds: one under his left eye, another in his left shoulder, another in his groin, and a long sear about four inches long on his skull. The men laid him on a soft blanket, expecting him to die. However, the superintendent began treatment right away, giving him injections and treating his wounds. Almost immediately Punch responded, much to the joy of his fellow soldiers. As soon as Punch was taken care of,

Judy the Boxer, who served in Palestine.

they turned their attention to Judy, who was covered in blood. They cleaned her and looked for wounds but only found a long graze on her back. They reasoned that Judy had laid on Punch to protect him and was covered in his blood. Both dogs recovered to live long lives.

A very big, black-furred Newfoundland dog named Gander was a mascot in the 1st Battalion, Royal Rifles of Canada. He is credited with saving the lives of several soldiers at the battle of Lye Mun on Hong Kong Island in December 1941. The Canadians' assignment had been to defend the island from the invading Japanese. On three occasions, Gander fought with his battalion. Because most of the battles happened at night, the Japanese could not see Gander. If they got too close to the Canadian troops, Gander would rush out and tackle them, charging out with a ferocious growl and biting at their heels as they ran away. It was on December 19, just after midnight, that the battle of Lye Mun broke out. Gander was with the soldiers, attacking the Japanese as needed. During one attack, a Japanese soldier threw a grenade at a group of seven wounded soldiers. Before anyone could do anything, Gander picked up the grenade and ran off with it, to his death. In October 2000, Gander was posthumously awarded the Dickin Gallantry Medal by the PDSA. The medal is on display in the Canadian War Museum in Ottawa. Gander was also honored by having his name included on the Hong Kong Veterans' Memorial Wall along with the other 1,977 Canadians who died in that battle. It is humorous that when the Japanese later interrogated their Canadian prisoners, they wanted to know about the "Black Beast." They had not realized it was a dog.

Some of the mascots who had been picked up in the North African Campaign made it back to Britain, some did not. Tocra was a cute Dachshund Terrier mix and had been a part of a German panzer group. She was adopted near Benghazi and became the mascot of the Second Army Signals Corp. She was beloved by all who knew her, and kept the soldiers' morale up and made them laugh.

Infantrymen of C Company, the Royal Rifles of Canada, and their mascot Gander the dog, en route to Hong Kong. This photo was taken in Vancouver, British Columbia, circa October 27, 1941. (Library and Archives Canada)

Then there was Shoofty, who was adopted by a senior officer in the Eighth Army. Shoofty loved to go on inspection with his master and would point out anyone who did not have their boots polished, or had other infractions, by laying down by the offender and wagging his tail. Even though the soldiers did not want to be singled out by Shoofty, they could not help but smile when he singled them out. When the officer was transferred, Shoofty was adopted by the cook and later returned to England with him.

The SS *Mekness* was a transport ship that set sail from Southampton, England, with more than 1,300 French marines on board. One marine had a white Labrador Retriever named La Cloche with him and the other passengers noted that nothing would lure the dog away from his owner. After several hours at sea, a German U-boat torpedoed the ship and La Cloche's master was thrown into the ocean, along with many other passengers. Unfortunately, La Cloche's master could not swim. La Cloche never took his eyes off his master and immediately dove into the water. He then swam to his master and grabbed his clothing, keeping his master's head above water to prevent him from drowning. It was quite some time before a boat was able to pull the unconscious French marine out of the water but before they could rescue La Cloche, a heavy sea swept the dog out of reach of the rescue boat. Everyone believed that he was lost. Fortunately, La Cloche found a sizable piece of wood and was able to climb onto it. He was eventually rescued and reunited with his master. Those who survived the incident never forgot his bravery. La Cloche was the first dog to be awarded the Blue Cross Medal by Our Dumb Friends' League.

Fo'c'stle was an Irish Terrier who sailed with the Royal Canadian Navy, and like many mascots, he was a real boost to the sailors' morale. When a U-boat wolf pack attacked the destroyer for five days straight, Fo'c'stle ran back and forth across the deck, barking. He even barked to alert the sailors of any U-boats that the ship's instruments had not detected. Day and night the attack continued. The crew got no rest and were so exhausted that they had difficulty responding to any alarm. Fo'c'stle kept the gunners alert by pulling on their trousers and barking at them. The ship survived the attack, but until the vessel reached port, Fo'c'stle stayed on the bridge to keep watch.

Lluda was a Cairn Terrier who had spent her early life on a North Sea fishing trawler. However, sometime between 1939 and 1940, she joined the Royal Navy and was assigned to a minesweeper as a part of the Dover Patrol. Lluda always stayed on the bridge and the sailors quickly learned that she had an amazing ability to detect enemy aircraft. When a plane, yet unseen and unheard by humans, was approaching from beyond the horizon, Lluda's body would start to shake and the hair on her back would stand up. Then, she would slowly turn and "point" with her head up and bark unceasingly. Within a few minutes the sailors, now at battle stations, would see a tiny speck in the sky as the enemy plane approached. They were ready and waiting. Interestingly, she would give the same "point" for friendly airplanes but would not bark. She was the best early-detection system the sailors had and they trusted her implicitly. Lluda finished her navy career in the mine-sweeping operation that preceded the commando raid on the Lofoten Islands in Norway. She had a long, happy life after her service in the military.

Bungie was a liver and white Springer Spaniel, owned by Flight Officer B. W. Lecky of the Women's Auxiliary Air Force (WAAF). He was a member of the Mascot Club. His rank in the service was flight sergeant and he was used to help recruit soldiers, an unofficial recruiting sergeant. When he joined the Mascot Club, he already had five years of service. His story started when he was orphaned after a bombing raid in South London. No one knew why but Bungie loved to fly; it was his preferred method of travel. Ground crews kept an eye on him when he was near the airplanes because he was often found climbing the wide rung ladder of a grounded RAF aircraft, whining to get into the cockpit. What made him rather endearing was his ability to sit up and salute, a trick he had learned while recruiting men and women.

After the war, Flight Officer Lecky was assigned to Berlin to work with the British Control Commission. This posed a problem since there were regulations about bringing dogs into Germany, but leaving Bungie behind was not an option for Lecky. Bungie weighed 45 pounds, and Lecky listed him as "Welfare Equipment and Props." On the way to the airport while on the bus, Lecky hid Bungie under the seat with a mackintosh draped carelessly over him. Once they arrived at the airport, Lecky could not hide Bungie. An officer approached the WAAF and walked along with her, telling her more than once that she could not take the dog. Lecky ignored the officer and did not reply. When Lecky stopped, Bungie looked up at the officer with soulful eyes and that did it: the officer walked away, saying no more. One hurdle overcome. Next, they had to pass through customs but ground staff sympathetic to the cause led them round the back, bypassing the customs office. Finally, they had made it to the airplane where, fortunately for them, the pilot was a dog lover. It helped that Bungie was wearing his coat with all his badges and decorations. Once on board, Bungie curled up in his basket and went to sleep until they reached Berlin. When they landed in Berlin, a very busy officer told Lecky that there were new regulations regarding dogs. Lecky then calmly told the officer that it was obvious he was unaware of the new regulations and that he'd better not find out about them until after they were gone. Bungie became as famous in Germany as he had been in England and toured far and wide, including Copenhagen. He had a long and successful career as a WAAF mascot.

Flight Sergeant Bungie.

Just Nuisance

Just Nuisance, a large Great Dane said to be 6 feet 6 inches tall when stood on his hind legs, was born in Rondebosch, Cape Town, South Africa, on April 1, 1937. His owner, Benjamin Chaney, ran the United Services Institute where the dog befriended all the sailors from the Simon's Town naval base. He then took to sleeping on the gangplanks of ships and would follow the sailors into Cape Town on the train, to accompany them back to base when the bars closed. He was adept at catching trains; if he missed one, he would either walk to the next station or simply wait for the next train. It was when the Cape Town Railways threatened to destroy the dog—he wasn't paying his fares and took up a whole bench seat—that the Royal Navy stepped in and enlisted him into the navy with the rank of able seaman, entitled to all benefits, including free train fares and rations. On the form, his surname was listed as "Nuisance" and because he didn't have a first name, the sailor with him wrote "Just." He was not an exemplary matelot: his charges included being AWOL, refusing to leave a bar at closing time, losing his collar, and sleeping in an officer's bunk (for which he forfeited seven days' bones). He did, however, appear at many promotional parades and events and was widely known in Cape Town. It is believed that somewhere along the line, Nuisance was hit by a car, which cased thrombosis and paralysis. On the advice of the naval veterinarian surgeon, he was put down on April 1, 1944.

Able Seaman Just Nuisance, the only dog to be officially enrolled in the Royal Navy during World War II. (Australian War Memorial/Wikimedia Commons)

Smudge was a black Retriever-type dog with a white chest and socks and was only 6 months old when he was enrolled in the Mascot Club. But at 6 months, he already had 45 hours of flying time in five different types of aircraft. He was stationed at Pocklington Air Station in Yorkshire and was the mascot for the entire squadron. Like most military personnel, the airmen felt that Smudge brought them luck because they held the record for the most number of flights (228) over Germany. Smudge was so valued by the men of the squadron that for his own safety he was only allowed to go on training flights. His principal airman was Flight Lieutenant H. L. Mackay, DFC, who was a mid-upper gunner.

Smudge's daily routine consisted of a morning run around the aerodrome, being doted on during the day, eating dinner at 8 o'clock, being brushed at night, and then sleeping next to Mackay's bed on a flight suit. At one point, Smudge caught distemper but was given the best of care and nursed back to health. Smudge had an uncanny way of knowing when Mackay was going on a mission. While Mackay was getting ready to leave, Smudge would mope about. Then, just as Mackay was ready to walk out the door, Smudge would lick his hand. He then would go to the window and press his nose against it as he watched Mackay walk out of sight. Sometimes he remained there for a very long time.

No one could explain how or why it happened but Smudge, usually eager to eat his dinner, dug into his bowl of food and then suddenly stopped eating. He then began looking at the door, growling, and walking around the room making a mournful noise. He eventually went over to the window where he always watched Mackay leaving, and after a few minutes, laid down with his head under his paws. The airman, Johnny, who was taking care of Smudge, and another friend noted the exact times that Smudge did this. Strangely, after 20 minutes of laying with his paws on his head, Smudge jumped up and shook himself, then started barking and wagging his tail before enthusiastically finishing his dinner.

Later that night Mackay returned, exhausted, wanting only to get some sleep, but Smudge would not leave him alone. He yanked at Mackay's clothes, licked his face, and refused to settle down. It took quite a while for Mackay to calm Smudge so that he could get some sleep. The next day Johnny told Mackay what had happened and the exact times of Smudge's strange behavior. It turned out that while on a bombing raid over Düsseldorf, Mackay's airplane had been hit by flak and caught fire. It had taken the crewmen 20 minutes to put the fire out. When Johnny and Mackay compared the times that the airplane had been hit and was on fire, the times corresponded exactly with Smudge's strange behavior.

Smudge knew his master was in trouble but no one could understand how he knew.

It seems that this type of behavior from mascots is not unknown. A red Cocker Spaniel named Buster also knew when his master was in danger. One night, after the aircraft had left for Berlin, Buster did not leave the airfield for nine hours. His master's bomber was the last to limp back to base, running on three engines with four wounded airmen on board.

Having the distinction of being the fifth member of the Mascot Club was a beautiful Collie pup named Wimpy. Sergeant Sylvia Lewis had found Wimpy at the WAAF Band at RAF Hereford. When she found him, he was about 2 months old and needed a bath and brushing to make him presentable. Wimpy's luxuriant coat flowed as he paraded in various towns for "Wings for Victory" and "Salute the Soldiers." He was a great attraction and people enjoyed petting him. He also did a great service to the RAF station by keeping the rat population at bay.

Beauty was a black German Shepherd who, as well as being a mascot, was a great guard dog at balloon sites. At night, she would guard the camp and not allow any unauthorized person near the site. One of the other jobs she had was to accompany the mail runner to fetch the mail. No one knew why, but Beauty loved cats and would try to groom them by licking them as a sign of affection. When the balloon units were split up, she went home with one of the aircraft women and settled into civilian life. It amazed WAAF members that even after she was mustered out, she would recognize and greet anyone who had been a WAAF.

Rats are always a problem at any military base, and no one complained when one day an elderly dog named Rover, who was about 11 or 12 years old at the time, appeared at a new air station near his home. Rover felt it was his duty to kill all the rats there and once he had cleared the base of rats, he then extended his search to a market garden and a local dump. He

Wimpy kept the rat population down at the RAF station.

Members of the 2/48th Battalion, 9th Australian Division, with a pet dog, after evacuation from Tobruk on the ship *Kingston*, October 1, 1941. (Flickr /Australian War Memorial Collection)

would arrive each morning, hunt rats, then return to the base in the evening, dirty, hungry, and tired. He was well cared for by the base personnel and his reputation grew. It took Rover about a year to clear all the rats from the base and the surrounding areas. He made sure that it would stay that way.

There is not much information about Anthony, a mixed black puppy who lived with the WAAFs at Hope Cove, Kingsbridge, Devon. What made him unusual was he really loved swimming, boating, and fishing. He had also obtained many flying hours, including operations or "OPs" over Germany and France. People loved to cuddle Anthony and they took him on fishing excursions. His enthusiasm was catching and he lifted many spirits.

Yanto was a Corgi with the Air Sea Rescue Unit stationed at Padstow, Cornwall. He was often seen waiting patiently for unit personnel to come ashore. He also loved fishing and would play with the fish and crabs hauled ashore in nets. Yanto knew the unit's routine well and always waited for the mobile canteen that came on Thursdays: he knew he would get a bit of chocolate and lots of love. He was a cheerful addition to the base.

Some mascots traveled extensively and Pat, a terrier mix, was one of them. Her owner, Sergeant Jimmy Russell, RAF, had purchased her when she was 18 days old while he was in Syria. When Pat was 6 weeks old, she and her master had deployed to Palestine and from there through the Sinai Desert to Egypt. At that point, Russell and Pat were serving at the front with a forward fighter squadron. From October 1941, until the Germans were pushed out of Africa, Pat and Russell served at forward airfields, advancing into Tripolitania (Libya),

Tunisia, Corsica, Sardinia, and then Italy, taking in Cairo, Alexandria, Tobruk, Derna, Benghazi, Tripoli, Tunis, Bizerta, Naples, and Rome, to name a few. Thanks to Pat's training as a war dog, he never faltered under fire or stress.

A Staffordshire Terrier, Judy, served in the Western Desert as a mascot for the Legal Department, RAF. She had taken it upon herself to guard headquarters, no matter where it was located. Judy was such a good guard dog that if she was not introduced to a new airman, she would consider him an intruder. A new airman was assigned to share a room with her master, Squadron Leader J. Barry. Barry had neglected to introduce Judy to the new man and when he tried to go to bed, Judy would not let him near it until her master returned and told her that it was OK. Fortunately, the new man had a good sense of humor and appreciated that after the introduction, he too would be protected.

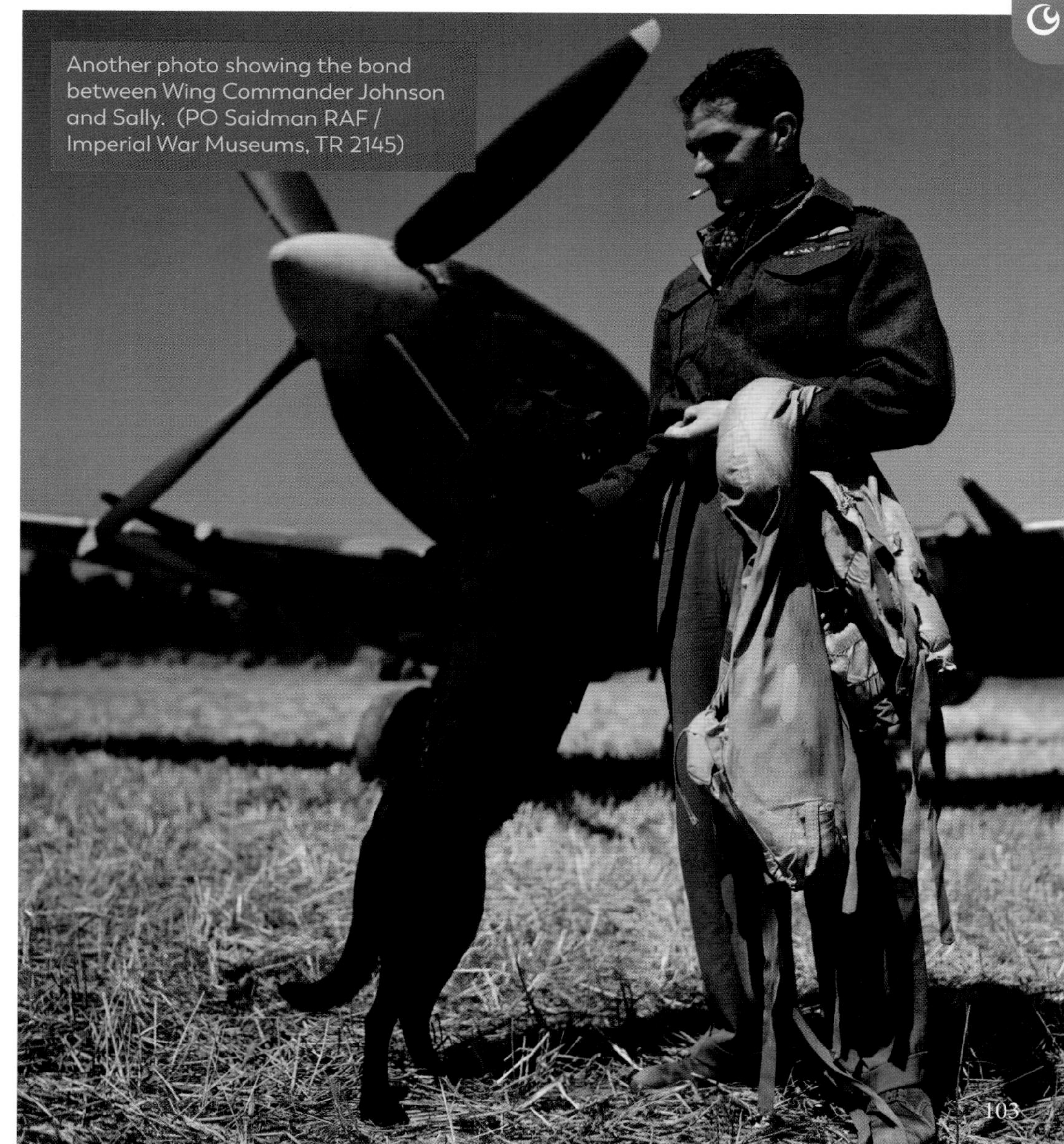

Another photo showing the bond between Wing Commander Johnson and Sally. (PO Saidman RAF / Imperial War Museums, TR 2145)

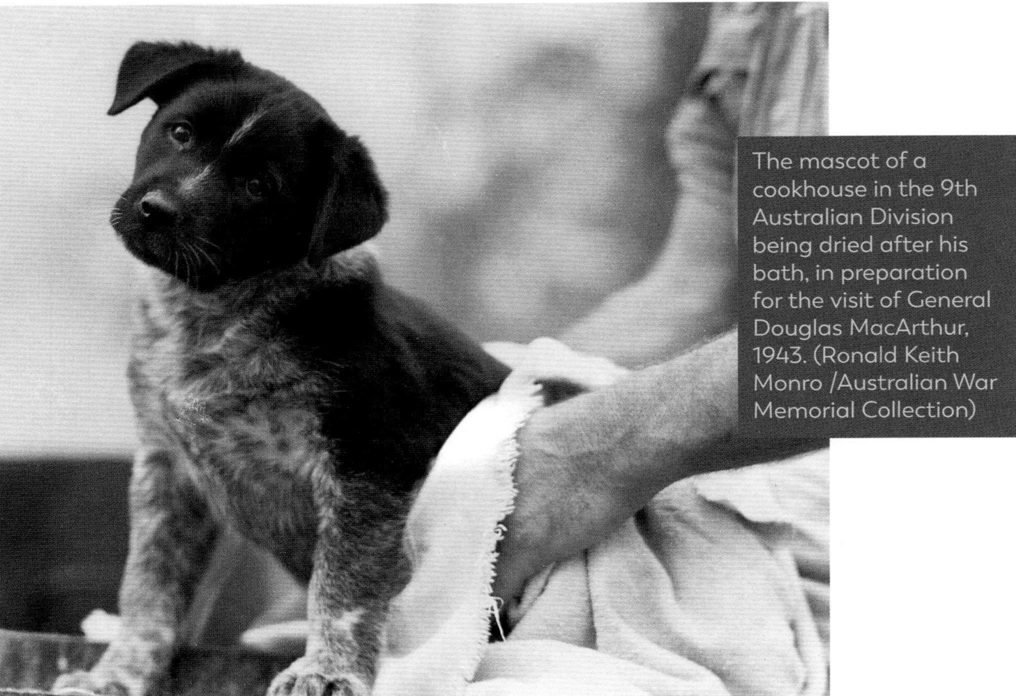

The mascot of a cookhouse in the 9th Australian Division being dried after his bath, in preparation for the visit of General Douglas MacArthur, 1943. (Ronald Keith Monro /Australian War Memorial Collection)

It is amazing what a dog might decide to do on his own without training. In the case of a tri-colored Collie named Bob, who was the mascot for the 193rd Railway Operating Company, Royal Engineers, this was the source of many laughs. Bob was well behaved and would accompany his master, Corporal L. C. Chapman, to church where he patiently lay under the pew. Bob also went to the theater with Chapman and had his own seat next to his master. If Bob saw dogs or cattle appear in a movie, he would sit up on his haunches, intent on the screen. Because this was humorous to the patrons, they would watch Bob instead of the movie. Often, if people knew that Bob was going to be at a movie, they would go just to watch him. Bob traveled with the railway crew and loved to ride in the engines, and sometimes he would be gone for days at a time. When the crew slept, he would guard them and not allow anyone near them. If any of the Egyptian laborers, who were noted for stealing, came near the men's tents, he would bite at their clothing, tearing it.

A South African soldier was laying severely wounded in a shell hole at Sidi Rezegh, during Operation *Crusader*, when a German Shepherd found him and started to lick his face and hands. When the medics found him and transported him to the field hospital, the dog refused to leave the soldier's side. No one knew if the dog belonged to the soldier or who the dog was. Out of compassion and because of the dog's devotion, the hospital staff took care of the dog while the soldier recovered. The soldier had no idea who the dog was or where he had come from, but on discharge, the dog was at his side and never left his new master. It was a complete mystery.

Fritz was a beautiful St. Bernard who belonged to a German soldier. The chain of events began with a fight between the British Royal Hampshire Regiment and the Germans at an Allied Mulberry Harbor (manmade mobile harbors used to unload men and materiel at Gold and Omaha beaches on D-Day). The two hills on either side of the harbor were duly captured by the Allies and when British troops entered the village of Arromanches, they were able to capture the last of the German soldiers who had been putting up resistance. As

Fritz, a St. Bernard captured from the Germans.

the Germans were marched off to a holding area, Fritz followed his master. It is not known how he got aboard the landing craft taking the prisoners to Southampton, but he did. When he was discovered as the vessel made port in England there was a problem due to quarantine restrictions. Initially Fritz was to have been destroyed, but a woman was so taken by his beauty that she offered to pay the quarantine fees.

After some time, the Hampshire officer who had captured the Germans learned that Fritz was in quarantine in England. He got in touch with the woman who had paid Fritz's fees and asked if the Hampshires could have him as a mascot. The woman agreed and Fritz became a beloved mascot of the regiment. He proudly took part in many parades, wearing a coat embroidered with the regimental crest and the names of the countries where the regiment had served.

When Corporal Tommy Mott found a very young puppy, barely old enough to be weaned, wandering the fields of Normandy, he named him Prince. Although very young, Prince stayed with the unit during the advance into France, a good thing because the soldiers had food to feed him (many abandoned dogs starved). For his first six weeks with the soldiers, Prince traveled constantly, curled up and shivering under the seat of a Jeep. Because the soldiers were regularly under shell and mortar fire, Prince learned what the whine of an approaching shell meant. He would then dive into a ditch or slit trench. As Prince grew, he became very good at sensing when a move was about to take place and long before it started he would parade by his truck, making sure that he was not left behind. After VE Day, the unit was stationed in Germany. Prince still insisted on going out with the trucks and if for some reason he was not allowed to, he would protest long and loud. In the winter, because of the cold, he was transferred to a Signals' store truck where he could stay warm. Prince loved to travel, and it was not unusual to see him riding on the hood of a car or the tank of a motorcycle when the weather was fine. The unit had several mascots, including a crow or jackdaw, a pigeon, a rooster, and a few rabbits. The crow would peck at Prince as he slept and would then share in his daily eggs. Prince was eventually found a home in North Rhine-Westphalia, where he settled in the town of Soest. He never lost his love of riding in a vehicle.

Two members of No. 31 (Beaufighter) Squadron, RAAF, holding the squadron mascots, a joey (young kangaroo) and a dog. From left: Flight Lieutenant G. A. Greenwood and Sergeant B. Agnew at Coomalie Creek, Northern Territory, 1943. (Flickr /Australian War Memorial Collection)

Flash was a cross Whippet and Irish Terrier and the mascot of the 443rd Battery, 61st Field Regiment, Royal Artillery; she had five years of service as a mascot. She traveled with her master, Gunner E. C. Duffield, and unit throughout England, Wales, and Northern Ireland. She was part of every battle, including the battle of Nijmegen. She knew the minute a German shell left its gun, and would dive for a slit trench. The soldiers knew to follow her immediately. At one point, the Germans located the British position and shelled it for hours while Flash gave comfort to the soldiers during those nerve-wracking moments. Flash developed a strong antipathy for Germans and would growl at prisoners when they marched by. On one occasion, fresh food ran short and the soldiers had to eat "iron rations," the preserved ration-pack food. However, Flash took it upon herself to provide several rabbits and hares for the men to cook. When it was time to go home, Gunner Duffield tried to get permission to bring Flash home to England with him. However, she was unlucky as the selection was on a lottery basis and she was not picked. Duffield wrote to the Mascot Club for help and because of Flash's record, they assisted with the expenses of the quarantine process. After six months, Flash was reunited with Duffield and they then enjoyed a long, happy civilian life together.

Sandy was a Border Terrier who served with the British Fourteenth Army in Burma. During his tour with the army, Sandy easily marched several thousand miles with the troops through jungles and swamps. He was always seen with the forward troops and with his master when it came time to make the rounds of the observation posts. Sandy was a great morale booster for the men, especially when things got tough. When the unit was ordered to attack and destroy a heavily fortified Japanese antitank section positioned up a 500-foot hill, Sandy was with the leading platoon and was hit during the bayonet charge, but that did not stop him. After the battle, Sandy spent time in the field hospital where he fully recovered. He then went back to his unit.

These brave dogs were able to navigate a shaky bamboo bridge. This team is on their way to attack the Namhkam village in Burma.

Wilhelm the Dutch Resistance Dog

There are not many accounts of dogs who helped the Underground, but one case has been recorded. This dog was a sheepdog named Wilhelm. His owner worked with the Dutch Resistance, sabotaging whatever he could by disabling railway carriages, attacking sentries, and gathering secret documents. On one occasion, Wilhem's owner was able to break into the German headquarters near the town of Appeldoorn and steal some important documents. Wilhelm was posted outside to stand guard while his master was inside. Suddenly, Wilhelm started to bark. His master quickly left the building and both dog and owner escaped into the woods. The Germans realized that someone had broken in and immediately initiated a massive search. When his master realized that they were almost surrounded, he opened the medical kit he carried and wrapped the documents in bandages. He then had wrapped the bandages as tight as he could around Wilhelm's body. He looked into the eyes of his faithful dog and ordered him to return home. The dog then disappeared into the night; he had to cross three rivers and travel a long distance. Days later, Wilhelm arrived at his home in Eindhoven, caked with mud and with a bullet wound to one of his hind legs. When he was cleaned up by his master's friends, they found the message in the bandage. Fortunately, Wilhelm recovered and was reunited with his master, who had managed to evade the Germans.

The USSR

Russians were very experienced in using dogs in war. During the Great Patriotic War of 1812, Russia had about 40,000 war dogs. By early World War II, the Soviet Union had trained over 50,000 dogs. The Red Star Kennels, also known as the Central School of Working Dogs under the direction of Colonel G. Medvedev, was responsible for producing those dogs. To Colonel Medvedev's credit, he had started a scientific breeding and training program to supply war dogs.

The breeds commonly used by the Russians were German Shepherds, Black Russian Terriers, Samoyeds, and other similar breeds. All the breeds selected had to be able to withstand harsh Russian winters. Most of the dogs initially came from dog hunting groups or dog clubs, and had been trained for several jobs. They pulled sleds with wounded soldiers, found mines, hauled ammunition, pulled soldiers on skis, and hauled equipment.

It was critical during the winter that wounded soldiers were found quickly, or they would not survive the cold. The dogs were instrumental in helping to find the wounded. This

With their dogs, Red Army dog handlers cycle past the podium during a Red Square May Day Parade, 1938. (ru.wikipedia.org)

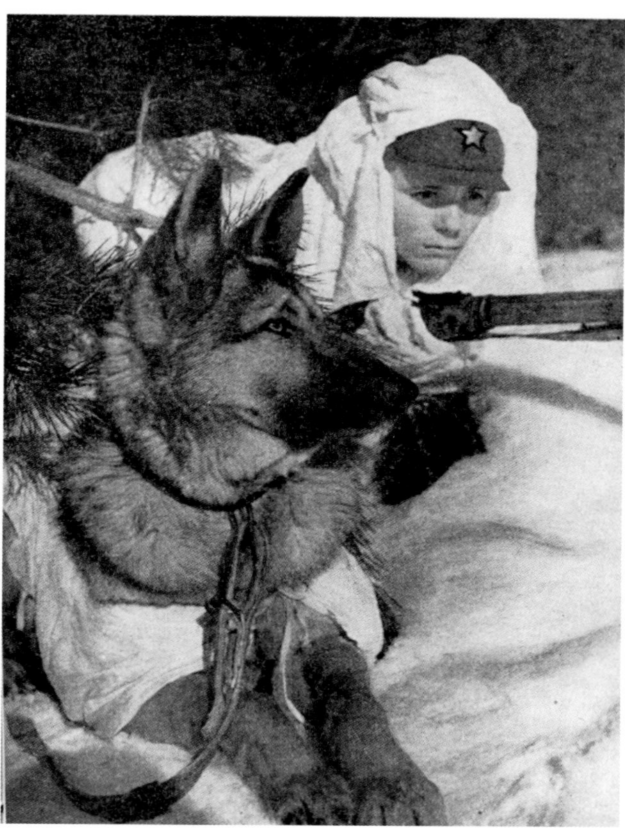

Russian dog in white camouflage vest.

became evident after a battle at Gzhatsk, a town near the Gzhat River in Russia. The snow was waist deep. Neither vehicles nor horses could reach the wounded soldiers laying in the snow. Sleds and sled dogs were used for rescue. In one sector, a team worked for five weeks and rescued a total of 1,239 soldiers. Each time the sled returned to the field of battle, it was loaded up with ammunition. That one team brought 327 tons of ammunition to the front lines. Samoyeds, because of their white coats, were used to pull sleds with troops in white camouflage up to the enemy lines. Seeing these Siberian troops, almost ghostly, was terrifying for the German soldiers. Soviet tactics were to send a barrage of machine-gun fire at the Germans and then quickly disappear.

Soviet dogs served as border guards, messengers, and wire layers. A team of six dogs was used to pull a sled mounted with a machine gun. A four-dog team transported medical supplies, and two dogs could pull a soldier on skis. The Russians had taught their guard dogs to attack anyone who tried to attack the dog's handler. The Russians also used antitank dogs, who were so successful that the Germans feared them. During a battle at the Kalinin

A Soviet POW and his pet, Finland, August 1941. (R. Stjernberg / Military Museum Finna CC BY-SA 4.0)

Russian sled dogs used to transport the wounded.

Front, Soviet troops were subjected to an artillery barrage to "soften" them up for a major attack. It wasn't long before a German panzer division came into view. As soon as the tanks were in position, the Germans heard an unusual sound: the sound of many barking dogs. Then, streaking toward them, came the Soviet antitank dogs. When the Germans realized that a pack of dogs was heading toward them, they turned tail and fled. The leader of the pack, a shaggy sheepdog named Tom, ran up to the first tank, leaped against the side, discharged the bomb which had been strapped to his body by pulling on a self-releasing belt, and then streaked away, unharmed. A few seconds later, the tank was a mass of smoldering, twisted metal.

The antitank dogs also proved their worth in the Lzyum Sector, a bulge or pocket south of the city of Kharkov, where the dogs destroyed nine heavy tanks, two armored cars, and killed all the men in each vehicle. Because many of the dogs could not run away fast enough and were injured or killed, the Soviet high command stopped using antitank dogs after the battle of Kalinin.

The Soviets used pack dogs similar to this Husky.

Awards Given to Dogs

The Order of Bagdan Khmelnitsky, the Order of Alexander Nevsky, and the Order of the Red Star were some of the awards that were given to dogs in the Soviet Union.

Dootik

A dog called Dootik was a mascot who brought aid to the crew of a Shturmovik, a "flying tank" or fighter-bomber. It is not recorded how Dootik helped the crew, only that he had done so.

Soviet military dog training school in Moscow Oblast, pre-1939. (Wikimedia Commons)

Bob

During a battle near Duminichi, an ambulance German Shepherd named Bob located 16 wounded men who had hidden themselves by crawling into ditches and shell holes. Bob would lay beside a wounded soldier and let the soldier access medical supplies from a pack on his back. If the man could not get up or use the medical supplies, the dog would return to the medics and then lead them back to the wounded man. One soldier tells how Bob saved him when he and a buddy were caught up in a bomb explosion. His buddy died but the soldier lived. He knew that he was badly wounded and so crawled into some brush, even though he realized it would make it more difficult for the medics to find him. Bleeding badly, he was starting to pass out when he felt a cold nose on the back of his neck. It was Bob. The soldier was unable to move, so Bob ran back to the medics for help. The soldier, almost unconscious, vaguely remembers being lifted onto the stretcher.

Soviet police dogs on parade, pre-1939. (Wikimedia Commons)

Barss

Barss was a mixed-breed dog attached to the Red Army on the Central Front. He had a reputation for being able to scent a German sharpshooter a mile away. Every time he scented an enemy sharpshooter, he would run in front of the Soviet soldiers and then stop about 50 feet away from where the sniper was hidden. Barss had hundreds of "finds" to his credit.

| The Axis

Germany

As stated earlier, Germany had a successful war dog program prior to 1914. After World War I the war dog program diminished, but by 1930, Germany had started to rebuild it in anticipation of going to war again. They established two war dog schools, one in Grunheide and one near Frankfurt, which could handle up to 2,000 dogs each. These schools were in violation of the terms of the 1919 Treaty of Versailles. The Germans claimed that the schools were used for training civilian and railway policemen. It may seem strange that animals were part of a peace treaty, but animals were a key factor during World War I. In large part, the dogs' tasks during World War I were to move materiel and supplies, send messages, and find the wounded. Because the Germans had planned to train war dogs before war broke out, they had the time to sort and test potential dogs for training. They started testing dogs at 6 months of age. Some of the criteria for determining whether a dog was suitable was the dog's ability to follow its handler over different terrain, climb stairs, enter dark rooms, cross ditches and other bodies of water, and be unafraid of gunfire.

This German dog is looking for people hiding to avoid deportation.

Wehrmacht Hungarian troops with their mascot, on parade, Ukraine, Eastern Front, 1942. (Fortepan CC BY 2.0)

Prior to World War II, the German dog training school had been run by an experienced World War I dog handler and trainer. Reichsbahninspektor (Reich Inspector) Langner understood the importance of matching the right dog with the right handler and favored handlers who were dog lovers. Every dog/handler team had to undergo a yearly inspection and if they failed, the team was broken up. Langner's methods were recognized worldwide.

Estonian Waffen-SS volunteer Kalju Jakobsoo from battalion Narva with his dog, Caesar, getting their photo taken for *Signal* magazine, 4 September 1944. (Julius Jääskeläinen CC BY 2.0)

A Waffen-SS handler and his dog, Norway, 1940. (Bundesarchiv CC BY-SA 3.0)

By the time Hitler came into power in 1933, the National Socialists had already formed training camps which included the Sturmabteilung (SA, the "Brownshirts") K9 units. These camps provided trained men for the new German Army and because the Germans had masked the training programs so well, by the time World War II started, Germany had over 200,000 dogs trained and ready for war. If that wasn't enough, Germany then publicized a call for more dogs which added another 100,000 to the ranks.

Primarily, the Germans used German Shepherds, Dobermans, Airedales, and Boxers. These dogs were trained to act as sentries, scouts, guards, and messenger dogs. Patrol dogs worked with their handler, accompanied by a patrolman who would check identity papers or perform other routine duties. The dogs in the Bahnschutz K9 units were also used to round up Jews and were used in ghettos as well as concentration camps to control, herd, and attack Jewish prisoners. Some 90 percent of the dogs used in this unit were German Shepherds. Throughout the war, prisoners, soldiers and Jews alike were forced to march in file, and dogs were used

A German patrol searching out partisans, 1939. (Niquille / Bundesarchiv CC BY-SA 3.0)

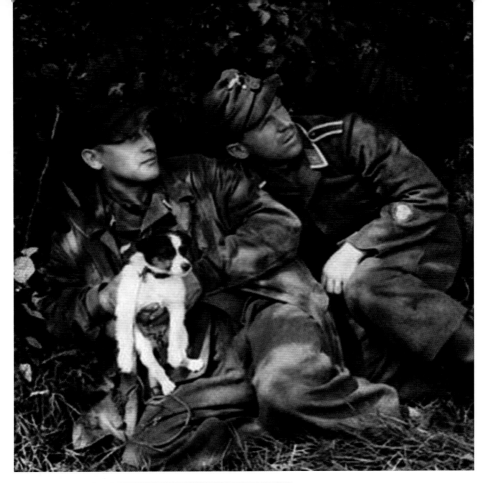

Luftwaffe troops and their dog taking cover in Normandy, June 1944. (Theobald & colorized / Bundesarchiv CC BY-SA 3.0)

A Waffen-SS recruitment poster appeals to Norwegian volunteers. (Artist Birger Cranner / https://norskeroster.wordpress.com/dnl/)

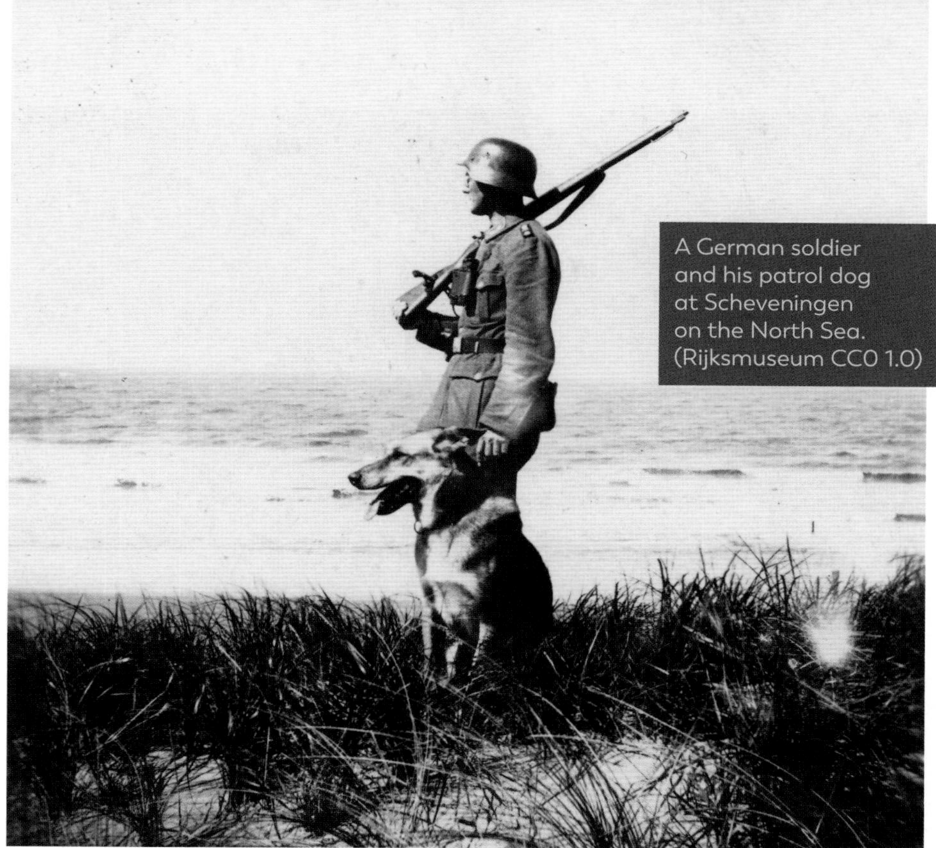

A German soldier and his patrol dog at Scheveningen on the North Sea. (Rijksmuseum CC0 1.0)

to keep them in line. If someone lagged or got out of formation, the dogs would nip them. These dogs were used in France, the Soviet Union, Italy, Poland, and North Africa in the same manner.

The Germans also used ambulance dogs. These dogs were trained to ignore any soldiers standing or walking. If a dog found a soldier lying on the ground, he would grab a short, detachable leather strap attached to his collar—called a *bringsel*—and go back to the handler. The handler would put the dog on a leash and the dog would lead the handler to the wounded soldier. For messenger dogs, the

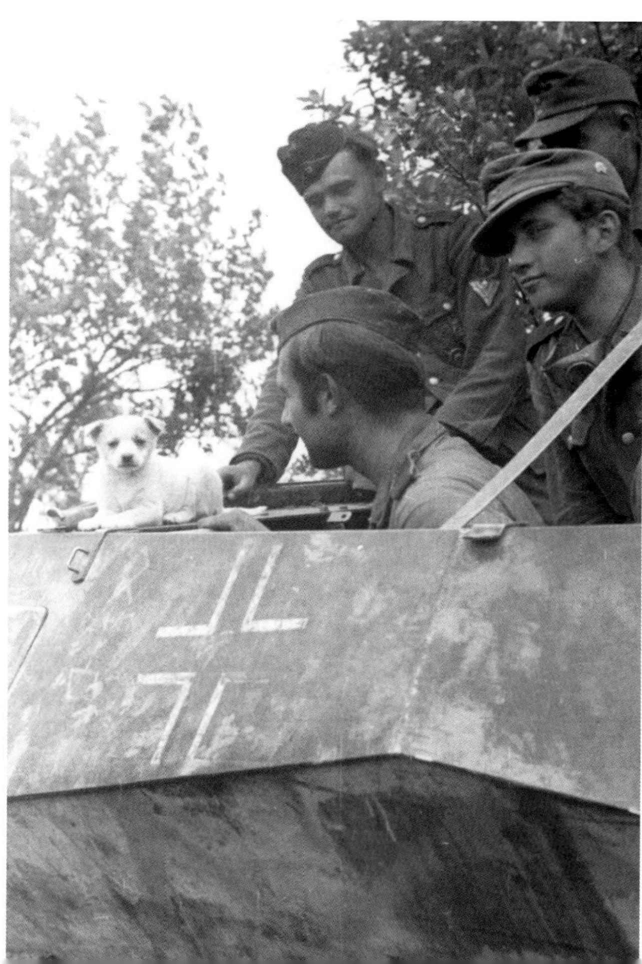

Panzergrenadiers on the Eastern Front with their mascot. (Krollpfeiffer / Bundesarchiv CC BY-SA 3.0)

Lieutenant-General Hahm (CDR 260th Infantry Division) and his dogs at Uspech, Russia, in May 1943. (Michael Korn / Wikimedia Commons {PD-US-expired})

Germans used only the smartest dogs. They taught the dog to follow a scent trail using a molasses-type scent that would be dispensed in a few drops every three feet. These dogs had one handler.

As dog lovers know, sometimes a well-trained dog will show a talent, or adapt to a task that goes beyond its training. There is an account of such an incident in North Africa that transpired between Allied and Axis troops, where, it seems, the Germans had taught pure white dogs to act as pointers. The Americans controlled the western part of a small valley in Ousseltria, Tunisia, while the Germans and the Italian forces controlled the eastern side. During the ensuing battle, dogs played an important part on both sides. When an American lieutenant and two sergeants were sent out to reconnoiter enemy positions, they spotted a pure white dog standing quietly and pointing. Within a few minutes, the Americans were raked with machine-gun fire. Later, when a patrol was sent out to look for the beleaguered Americans, the dog was gone. The dog's job had been to show the Germans where the enemy soldiers were located. This was not the only time American soldiers saw pure white dogs pointing out their positions and then returning to the Germans. Sadly, when the Germans and Italians had to withdraw quickly from Africa, they abandoned most of their dogs. Throughout the war, the Germans used so many dogs that there were few left for breeding stock after it ended.

Japan

Just as the war dog program in Britain appealed to its citizens to donate their dogs for the war effort, so too did Japan appeal to her citizens to donate their dogs for military service. To assist with this, they glorified an account that took place during their war with China before the attack on Pearl Harbor.

In an article by James Simpson, "The Canine Heroes of the Imperial Japanese Army," published in *War is Boring* (February 6, 2014) he explains that in order to convince the general population to donate their dogs, the Japanese glorified the story of *Major Itakura and His Loyal Dogs*, a propaganda account written by Genichi Kume in 1932. According to the account, which is not entirely accurate, Itakura was the trainer/caretaker of his unit's dogs. His favorite dogs were three German Shepherds, Meri, Nachi, and Kongo. At the time, the Japanese were at war with the Chinese and Private Ueno was handling Meri. When Ueno was wounded by shrapnel, he could not hold on to Meri, who ran into the middle of the battle. At a different location, Kongo and Nachi had also disappeared. After the battle, Itakura searched for the three dogs but could not find them. Eventually, the bodies of the dogs were found. They had been shot and killed by Chinese soldiers. The Japanese used a dramatization of the account to target schoolchildren, telling them that the dogs "died a death that is heroic beyond comparison" to teach the children to have a tough and

Japanese infantry and war dogs in action, China, 1938. (JACAR)

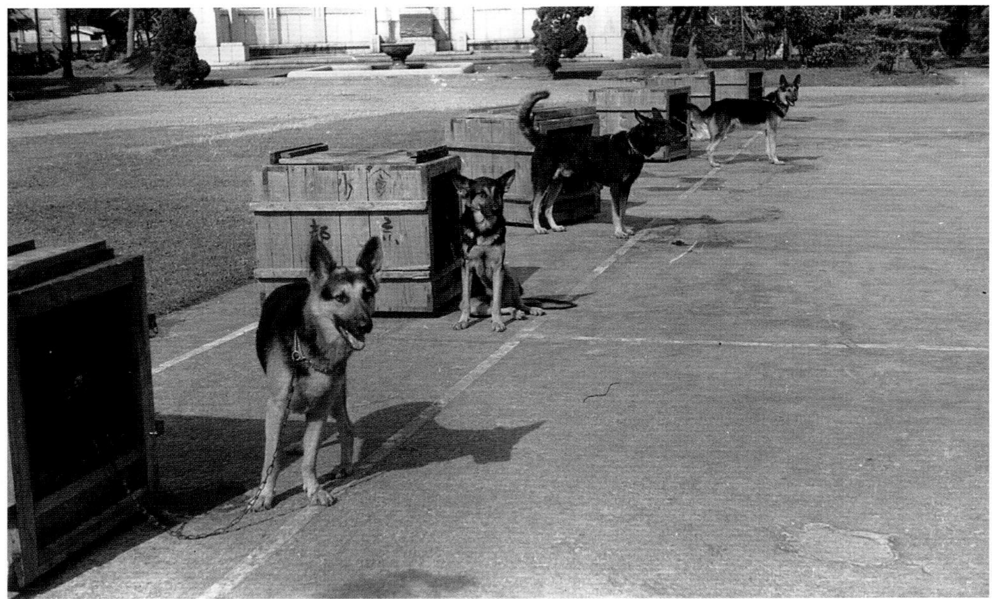

Training of Japanese military working dogs in Taihoku, 1940–1. (Wikimedia Commons {PD-US-expired})

courageous spirit. This story was the inspiration that kept the military dog program going in Japan, as well as subsequent stories in the media of dogs fighting for the emperor. However, dogs were still considered working animals and by and large not kept as pets.

Before Japan attacked Pearl Harbor, they had already built up their army to a war footing and were engaged in a war of conquest with China. Their German allies had supplied Japan with about 25,000 trained dogs. Most were German Shepherds, the breed that the Japanese seemed to prefer. The Japanese then set up several dog training schools in Japan and one in Nanking, China.

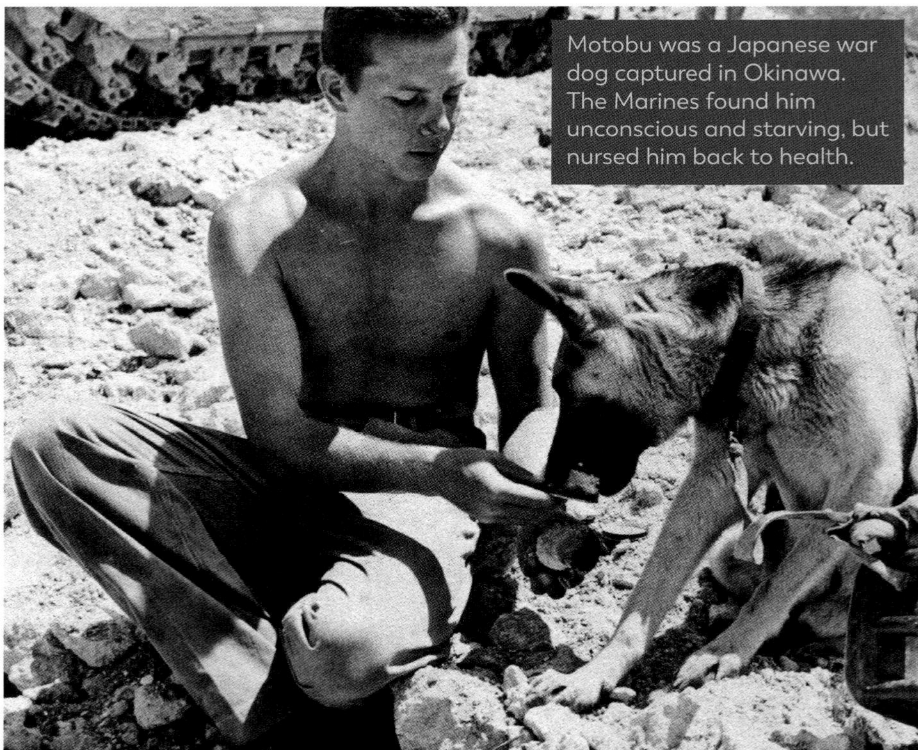

Motobu was a Japanese war dog captured in Okinawa. The Marines found him unconscious and starving, but nursed him back to health.

Imperial Japanese Army dog training, Formosa, 1940–1. (Wikimedia Commons {PD-US-expired})

The Japanese used dogs for patrols, as scouts, and as sentry dogs. They also used them as suicide dogs. Instead of trying to blow up tanks as the Russians had tried to do, the Japanese had the dogs pull small carts loaded with bombs onto American positions. Once the carts were close enough, the Japanese would detonate the cart. The Japanese also used untrained, vicious dogs in various campaigns and let them attack soldiers and civilians alike, as was the case in Hong Kong.

Interestingly, the Japanese had also tried to use small mixed-breed dogs to locate enemy troops, in much the same way as the Germans used the white dogs trained to point. Instead of pointing, the small dogs would search an area and once they located the enemy, would

IJA Youth Army troops training with military dogs, Taihoku, 1940–1. (Wikimedia Commons {PD-US-expired})

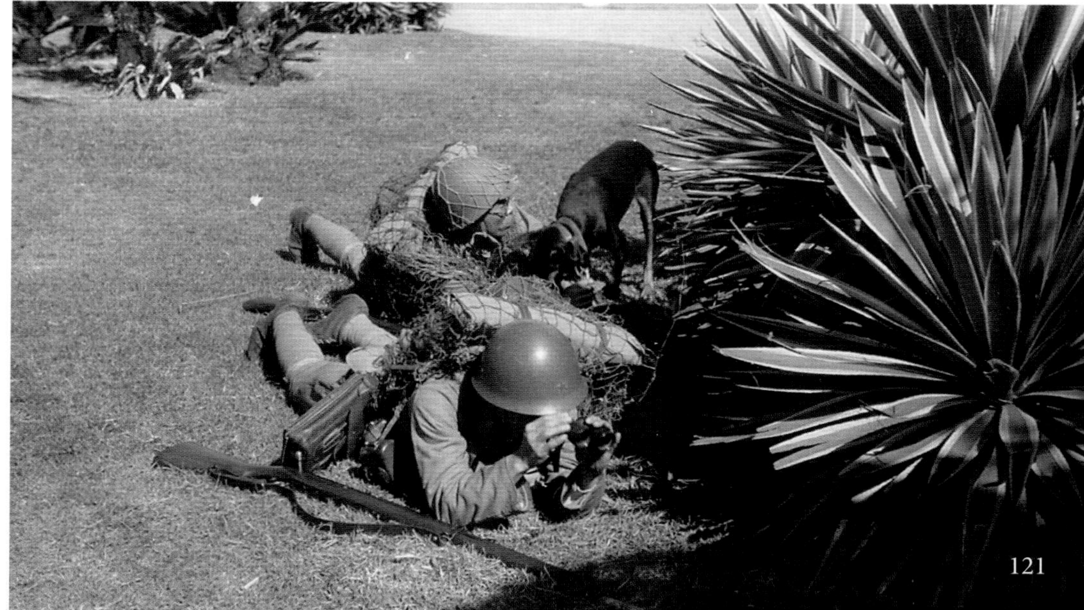

run back to the Japanese to alert them to the American positions. These dogs were not vicious, but the Americans soon figured out what the dogs were doing and would instead follow them back to the Japanese positions. The soldiers who encountered Japanese war dogs often commented that the dogs were, for the most part, poorly cared for; they were not well groomed, were half-starved, and had not been well trained. The Japanese used the typical village street mongrel as patrol and messenger dogs. Not many of the purebred dogs that were owned by the more affluent members of Japanese society were donated for the war effort.

One of the more famous dogs in Japan was a German Shepherd named Nikko, after the town where she was born. A statue of Nikko is in the center of what was the Japanese dog training school in Nanking. After the battle of Kiukiang, on the Yangtze River in China, the Japanese Canine Corps sent out several dogs to the front lines. Because telephone lines were down, messages had to be sent via messenger dog. One of the Japanese commanders needed to send a very important message to his headquarters, and decided to entrust it to Nikko. Before Nikko took off, she gently wagged her tail and licked the commander's hand. Then she sped into the night, past shell holes and explosions, barbed wire, and bursts of gunfire from both sides. At dawn, the soldiers awaited reinforcements but Nikko did not return. Later, her body was found. She had been shot and the Japanese soldiers mourned her loss. They took locks of her fur, some of which are enshrined in the statue honoring her. The Japanese awarded their hero dogs the Order of the Golden Kite.

Imperial Japanese Army dog Saburo. (Wikimedia Commons)

After World War II, dogs were still not kept as pets. According to Steven Givens in an article which appeared in *Nikki Asia* (February 15, 2023), it wasn't until the 1960s that the Japanese allowed their dogs to live indoors with them. Prior to that, dogs were kept on short chains at the entrances of buildings and houses for protection purposes. The Japanese did not breed dogs as companions but solely for work. However, in the 1960s the Japanese people changed their attitude toward dogs. There were several reasons for this: Japan became more prosperous after World War II; a more Westernized lifestyle took hold; movies featuring dogs became popular, such as *Lady and The Tramp*; and lastly, the fertility rate and average family size dropped.

Going Home

After World War II ended, Britain continued to use their war dogs to locate mines, guard prisoners and military posts, as well as stockpiles of fuel, food, and vehicles, which all had to be protected.

One incident spoke of a dog named Roy, who disappeared while clearing mines. Seven weeks and 40 miles farther down the line, he reappeared. Apparently, he had followed the scent of other dogs and their workers and had aided them in locating mines. When he returned, he was in poor health, but made a full recovery.

In the Mediterranean, guard dogs had earned quite a favorable reputation. A German Shepherd named Blackie prevented eight Italian thieves from stealing from a clothing store. He pinned the leader of the group against a wall and randomly snapped at the others. A Boxer named Piggy attacked four local thieves in Cairo but lost an eye in the confrontation. However, this did not stop her and she was able to return to duty once she recovered. Snook, a Doberman Pinscher, was blown up by a landmine in Egypt while chasing thieves, but made a full recovery. Five other dogs, Jerry, Prince, Shelia, Ran, and Lilith, also worked as guard dogs and prevented thefts of military and civilian property.

Guard or patrol dogs were still used at POW camps after the war. Many owners who had donated their dogs to the war dog effort did not want their dogs back. These dogs were retrained to guard prisoners or to perform other military duties. As soldiers were sent home, the vast number of mascots and war animals became a problem. To bring a dog home required a special license from the military veterinary authorities—after World War I, when soldiers were allowed to bring their animals home, there had been an outbreak of rabies. Dogs that were slated to be reassigned to military posts in Britain were sent home with no issues. Cats could be brought home under quarantine if they were privately paid for. No other animals were allowed to be brought home.

Barty was owned by a French doctor and after a raid on his village, Benkovac, British soldiers went to inspect the village. Major Dupont found Barty and located his owner. The doctor told the major that he could not feed Barty and allowed the major to take him. Barty traveled with the major to Yugoslavia, and when the war ended, Dupont managed to bring Barty home.

Smoky, the Yorkshire Terrier, found abandoned in a foxhole in the New Guinea jungle.

This account closes with the story of Smoky, a Yorkshire Terrier who a soldier found abandoned in a foxhole in the jungles of New Guinea. The soldier sold her to William A. Wynne for about $6. Smoky weighed 4 pounds and stood only 7 inches tall. For the rest of the war she traveled in Wynne's backpack, accompanying him to the jungles of New Guinea and the Rock Islands. Because she was not a military dog, she did not receive any of the medical care or military rations available to war dogs. Despite the lack of military status and care, she remained healthy. According to Wynne, she served in the South Pacific with the 26th Photographic Reconnaissance Squadron, Fifth Air Force, flying 12 air/sea rescue and photographic reconnaissance missions. She took part in 12 combat missions and earned eight battle stars. She also survived 150 air raids, and one typhoon at Okinawa.

She is credited with saving Wynne's life by warning him of incoming shells while on a transport ship. She was the first official therapy dog and performed in various hospitals. Because of her small size and courageous attitude, during the Luzon campaign, she was used by the Signal Corps when they needed to run a telegraph wire through a 70-foot-long pipe of only eight inches diameter. Parts of the pipe were filled with soil up to four inches high. Wynne tied a string to Smoky's collar that was attached to the wire and sent her through the pipe. She successfully accomplished her task, saving around 250 ground-crewman from days of being exposed to enemy fire to otherwise lay the wire.

After the war, Smoky and Wynne continued to visit hospitals and she became a national celebrity featured in newspapers and local TV shows. She died at the age of 14. There is a monument in her honor at the Cleveland Metroparks, Rocky River Reservation in Lakewood, Ohio, that marks the place where she is buried. Other monuments have been dedicated to her. Smoky was awarded the PDSA Certificate for Animal Bravery of Devotion in April 2011 and received the Animals in War and Peace Distinguished Service Medal in 2022.

Sources & Further Reading

A Special Presentation from Hahn's 50th AP K9, West Germany, "WWII Combat: Axis and Allies" www.k9history.com/WWII-combat-soviets-axis.htm.

"Animals Were Allies Too" in *National Geographic*, Vol. 89, No. 1, January 1946.

Barrow, Mandy, "Introduction to Rationing During WWII" in *Primary Homework Help* www.primaryhomeworkhelp.co.uk/war/rationing.htm.

Behan, John M. *Dogs of War*, Charles Scribner's Sons, New York, 1946.

"Buddies: Soldiers and Animals in World War II" in *Prologue* magazine, Fall 1996, Vol. 28, No. 3 www.archives.gov/publications/prologue/1996/fall/buddies.html.

Bulanda, Susan. *Soldiers in Fur and Feathers: The Animals that Served in World War I - Allied Forces,* Alpine Publications, 2014.

Campbell, Clare, *Dogs of Courage: When Britain's Pets Went to War 1939–45*, Corsair, London England, 2015.

Dempewolff, Richard, *Animal Reveille*, Doubleday & Company, Inc., New York, 1946.

Dogtime, Mike, "Five Famous War Dogs" by Mike Dogtime, https://dogtime.com/dog-health/general/10959-five-war-dogs-for-memorial-day, retrieved January 2020

Dong, Shihao Tao Lin, James C. Nieh & Ken Tan, "Social Signal Learning of the Waggle Dance in Honey Bees" in *Science*, 2023, DOI: 10.1126/science.ade1702.

Downey, Fairfax, *Dogs for Defense: American Dogs in the Second World War 1941–45*, Daniel P. McDonald, New York, 1955, by the Direction and Authorization of the Trustees Dogs for Defense, Inc.

Forces, Alpine Publications, Colorado, 2014.

Gilroy, James, *Furred & Feathered Heroes of World War II*, Trafalgar Publications, Great Britain, 1946.

Going, Clayton, *Dogs at War*, The Macmillan Co., New York, 1946.

https://dogtime.com/dog-health/general/10959-five-war-dogs-for-memorial-day.

https://warfarehistorynetwork.com/2016/11/09/the-dogs-of-war/.

Lemish, Michael, G., *War Dogs: Canines in Combat*. Brassey's, Washington & London, 1996

Letts, Elizabeth, "The Perfect Horse: The Daring U.S. Mission to Rescue the Priceless Stallions Kidnapped by the Nazis" in https://nypost.com/2016/08/20/why-us-troops-risked-their-lives-in-wwii-to-rescue-horses-kidnapped-by-nazis/.

Lubow, Robert E., *The War Animals*, Doubleday & Company, Inc., New York, 1977.

Richardson, E. H. Lieutenant-Colonel, *Fifty Years with Dogs*, Hutchinson & Co. London post-1938 n.d.

Richardson, E. H. Lieutenant-Colonel, *War, Police and Watch Dogs*, William Blackwood & Sons, London, 1910.

Richardson, E. H. Lieutenant-Colonel, *Watch Dogs: Their Training and Management*, London: Hutchinson & Co., 1924.

Saunders, Blanche, *The Story of Dog Obedience*, Howell Book House, 1974.

Shute, Joe, "Unsung Heroes: The Brave Dogs Who Fought WWII," in *The Telegraph*, September 26, 2015 www.telegraph.co.uk/history/world-war-two/11891922/Dogs-of-war-the-unsung-heroes.html.

St. Hill Bourne, Dorothea, *They Also Serve*, Winchester Publications Limited, London, 1947.

The United States War Dog Association, Inc., "Types of War Dogs" , https://www.uswardogs.org/war-dog-history/types-war-dogs/, Retrieved February 2020

Turbak, Gary, "Saluting Canine Courage" in *VFW* magazine, February 2000.

TM 10-396 War Dogs, July 1943.

"Warfare History: The Dogs of War", https://warfarehistorynetwork.com/2016/11/09/the-dogs-of-war/, retrieved February 2020

"World War II Combat: Axis and Allies," www.k9history.com

www.uswardogs.org/war-dog-history/types-war-dogs/.

Young, Thomas, *Dogs for Democracy: The Story of America's Canine Heroes in the Global War*, Bernard Ackerman, Inc. New York, 1944.

"Your Dog Joins Up" in *National Geographic*, Vol. 83, No. 1, January 1943.

Index